Lenin as Organic Centralist

Organic Centralism In Lenin, The Left And Actual Party Life

Foreword

The Communist Party was born in 1848, based on a definitive theory of revolution and a fundamental outline of tactics. In the following decades Marx and Engels sculpted, in a powerful and masterful work, the fundamental theoretical corpus of Communism, a doctrine that is also called, to better restrict the doctrinal reference, Marxism. This work has never ended, carried on by the great Marxists and their schools, and which continues today within our small but obstinate formation.

In the meantime, the physical organization of revolutionaries, the Communist Party, went through a series of organizational forms, also undergoing an evolution, though sometimes with ruinous degenerations; its very name had been abandoned, until being recovered by the Bolsheviks of Lenin in 1918.

In 1973 the Party found it necessary to confront its history, to receive confirmation that it was fully in the tradition of the Communist Left (also known as the Italian Left), the current which, after having founded in 1921 the Communist Party of Italy (Section of the Communist International), was ousted and then expelled because of its unwillingness to silently accept the methods and policies of Stalinism, triumphant in the International.

An organic work was published under the title "The Communist Party in the Tradition of the Left".

To that work we therefore refer the comrades who intend to deepen their knowledge of the structure, functioning and tactics of the International Communist Party. The work is available online and as a printed volume also in English, French, and Spanish.

The text was compiled from the corpus of texts, articles, theses that the Left had produced in over half a century, a rich mass of documents accumulated since the early post-war period. Lenin's texts were also planned to be used, especially those from the years of the formation of the party, but it was not possible, for reasons of opportunity and time, to support the work with the rich theoretical production of Comrade Lenin, who had dedicated many of his energies to the construction of a true revolutionary party: a work, among other things, that allowed the Bolshevik Party to lead to victory the workers and peasants masses in the revolution that had its epilogue in Russia in October 1917.

Unfortunately, the need to demonstrate within the old organization, in a reasonably short time, to the dazed and deceived comrades, but also to ourselves, who had remained "on the road of ever", in the wake of the tradition of the Left, did not allow then to include in the publication the texts of Lenin that we were ordering. Comrade Angelo, who had taken charge of them and undertook this second part of the study, unfortunately passed away in 1978, and his work remained the notes (and many underlinings in the volumes of the Collected Works), which however proved to be precious for the start of the work we are presenting here.

At any rate, it has always been a certainty, in the hearts and minds of all comrades, that we were the true and only heirs of Lenin's and the Bolsheviks' work, also and above all thanks to the way the Party and its internal life were conceived.

From this conviction was born this work, which like all our work is impersonal and collective, and which consists of a collection of selected Lenin's writings and some other sources, on the one hand, and the writings of the Left and the unwritten rules of behavior and work of the Party today, on the other. The result, as the comrades will see, if the obvious differences linked to the era and environment in which Lenin's writings were produced are taken into account, is exactly what was intended to be verified; and it could not be otherwise. The objectives are the same, the demands linked to the work according to the right revolutionary policy, are the same. Identical is the passion that then and now guided and guides revolutionaries of all latitudes, ethnicities and languages.

The work is dedicated especially to the young comrades who in recent years have approached the party from countries where the tradition of communism has long been forgotten, mystified, or condemned. To these comrades, who contribute to making the party more and more international, the wish for good work, in the uncorrupted track of the revolutionary Marxism of all time.

1. Historical Invariance of the Communist Party

This work aims to demonstrate what we have affirmed since the birth of the party: alongside the claim of a doctrine that is unique and intangible since the enunciation of its theoretical foundations with the Communist Party Manifesto of 1848, we claim that just as the doctrine has been transmitted intact to this day, the way of conceiving the party of the communist revolution is also that of our teachers.

Already Marx and Engels, throughout their lives, had bitterly and fiercely condemned, both in the party's first embryonic and undeveloped form, and then in the developed ones, any improper attitude with respect to its nature, its tasks, and the aims of communism. Well known is their surprise and disgust at the attitudes of some anarchists, for example, and, in their hard work, they never descended to unworthy methods of political struggle, contrary to the conviction and help to the collective maturation of the world movement. We anticipate here a central thesis: The Communist Party engages in an external political struggle against its many enemies; not an internal struggle, except in case of irreparable degeneration. There are no polemics and no propaganda among comrades within the party. Lenin was eventually able to design and build a party that lived up to its historical task, not only , as is evident, from the point of view of theory, but also regarding its organizational structure and organic functions, aspects nevertheless never addressed separately.

That Lenin's party was, in the substance of the guidelines and of the way of conceiving the work, the same of the Left, before and after the Second World War, taking into account the obvious differences of time and place, has always been a deep-rooted belief in the party, and an obvious consequence of doctrinaire homogeneity. This belief was confirmed over 50 years ago in an internal circulation letter, written by the Party Center at the time: *"Our enemies have always wanted to oppose Lenin to the tradition of the Left, not only in the field of organizational matters, but in all fields. Our effort, however, ... has always been to discover the permanent Lenin under the contingent Lenin, to show how the "new type" party that he has been able to create in antithesis with the social democracy of the Second International already represents the Party as we conceive it, and how a truly organic method already emerged behind the formula of democratic centralism - which is to be seen not in the individual solutions given by Lenin to individual contingent problems, but in the continuity of his action. We must therefore deal with this issue by giving greater importance to the historical method, and bearing in mind how the transition from the second phase of the maturation of the class party, in relation to the development of capitalism, to the third phase, which is both that of the imperialism and of our party. Linked to this defect of a-historicity ... there is that of considering the organizational problems as stand-alone. Instead, it must be demonstrated how the centralism of the Bolshevik party was achieved through a struggle for the program, principles, and tactics of communism, before and after the II Congress of 1903."* (Letter from the center to the restricted network, 24/3/1967).

Our party therefore claims total continuity with the purest revolutionary tradition of the working class, originating with the Communist Manifesto of 1848, passing through the most orthodox (in the Marxist sense) expressions of theory and action within the three Internationals; and proclaims himself direct heir of the Communist Party of Italy, founded in 1921 and with which it also boasts an uninterrupted physical continuity, as concerns organization and men, champions for over a century of the uncorrupted tradition of leftist revolutionary communism.

2. Reasserted confirmations from a great past

While never losing contact with the working class and its daily struggle, it is our tradition to devote great energy, in times when direct revolutionary attack is impossible, to the study of the theoretical bases of our way of existing and to operate, both to continually reappropriate it, and to continue in the work of sculpting our positions in doctrine and tactics; which does not mean "enrichment", "updating" or, worse, "revision", but rather the highlighting of increasingly clear and detailed confirmations of the validity of our way of interpreting the revolutionary process.

We firmly believe that the doctrine of the revolution is not "built" by subsequent contributions and additions, in a process that would never be considered finished, and therefore susceptible to continuous "improvements" and "updates", in the light of alleged "new conditions", previously unpredictable. The doctrine of the revolution, which is formed on the basis of historical, economic, scientific, philosophical data, and also following utopian theorizations of future society, was born in a single block in the first half of the nineteenth century, and sees the light in the form of the Communist Manifesto. Nothing new is added in the 170 years following this theoretical body which contradicts its assumptions, if not continuous "sculptures" made by true Marxists, which make the instrument of theory more and more manageable and effective. The party therefore, to the shame of the hesitant and the doubtful, is always ready to play its role, with all the tools it needs, none excluded, to be applied to the disruptive and invincible force of the proletariat.

Consequently, the party is at the same time the custodian of the doctrine and the organ which, according to it, will have to carry out a leading role for the revolutionary class. It is therefore important for us to pay particular attention to this organ of the working class even when the class, in the vast majority of its components, ignores it, as in the present moment.

3. The formation of the Bolshevik Party

The International Communist Party is not only the heir of the Italian Left; it is our understanding that there are no substantial differences between our way of understanding the party and that of Lenin, obviously after having appropriately assessed the historical and environmental differences between the situations in which the two organizations have found themselves operating. This work intends to read the experience of Lenin and his party, underlining the characteristics which are of general value, the same of our small movement today.

To understand what the revolutionary party meant to Lenin, and to correctly interpret its position, it is essential to have a clear context in which Lenin operated, especially in the period of defining what the Bolshevik party would have been, before and after the II congress of the Russian Social Democratic labor Party (RSDLP). A brief historical premise is therefore necessary that allows us to define the characteristics of the various political actors, of movements and ideologies that circulated in Russia at the turn of the nineteenth and twentieth centuries.

Lenin gives us a description of the origins of the party in Russia both in the conclusion of the *What is to be done?* and in the preface to the *Twelve Years* collection (1907).

It was in the 1880s that Marxism penetrates Russia, where the populist movement had developed. The Emancipation of Labor group is established abroad around Marxist theory and with correct propositions on the tactics of the proletariat in the double revolution.

Lenin, in *What is to be done?* claims that that group possessed not only theory but had also developed a tactical plan for the perspective of the Russian revolution and the function of the proletariat in it.

In the first period, 1880-1898, the struggle of the Marxists took place above all against populism, a political movement that developed in Russia between the last quarter of XIX century and early XX; its aim was to achieve, through the propaganda and proselytism carried out by intellectuals among the people and with a direct terrorist action, an improvement of the living conditions of the lower classes, in particular of the peasants and serfs, and the realization of a kind of rural socialism based on the Russian rural community, in contrast to western industrial society. To settle up with this doctrine not only authentic Marxists intervene, but also a whole series of characters for whom the criticism of populism means need for a passage to bourgeois democracy. It is the era of Legal Marxism.

The struggle is therefore waged on two fronts: against populism and against petty bourgeois Marxism, and the first socialist writings are dedicated to this struggle, mainly by Lenin and Plekhanov. The date 1890, Lenin's debut in the political arena, simply coincides with this: the appearance of the working class in Russia. In this era, Russian Marxists are reduced to a small group; what Lenin writes in *What is to be done?* is important: this group of intellectuals had already worked out everything; they did not wait for "the masses".

The first, notable workers' unrest occurred in 1896, and the group of intellectuals threw themselves into the struggle, indicating to the movement not only its immediate tasks, but also all its perspective up to socialism.

The effects of this and subsequent movements were as follows: 1) the party joined the class; 2) the party separated clearly from legal Marxism; 3) the party organization was formed (1898).

Lenin states in all his works, including *What is to be done?* that from 1896 onwards the Russian proletariat was never static. The situation was that the party organization was inadequate to guide the lively movement of the working masses. So, the question is posed in *What is to be done?* where the crucial problem is precisely: how must the party suitable to lead the workers' movement be? It is in the face of this exuberant workers' movement that the economist deviation manifests itself.

This is a first characteristic trait that must be noted if we truly believe that the party is a product and a factor of class struggle. The difficulties towards the formation of a revolutionary party must be seen in the particular situation of Russia compared to other industrialized countries, or on the way to industrialization. The workers were very few in percentage, and concentrated in some industrial districts; the rest of the vast country was a large countryside with small and medium-sized farmers (in addition to large estates wage laborers or former serfs), from whose ranks came the generation which at the turn of the century constituted the industrial proletariat. Trade union tradition was almost non-existent, as was socialist propaganda. The revolutionaries therefore had to speak to a predominantly illiterate and suspicious audience.

A condition, however, that could reveal positive aspects; indeed not even the opportunistic poison had penetrated much into the class, and it was easier to put the proletarians in front of the reality of their conditions, and to help them to draw valuable indications from the struggles as to who were the friends and who the enemies. On the other hand, the bourgeois-oriented opportunism of a bourgeoisie that had to be revolutionary towards absolutism did not have the weapons typical of opportunism, or had little of it: propaganda, traditions, electoralism. It was therefore an opportunism with little theoretical tools, although rapidly evolving, even within the socialist movement, and also thanks to the development of opportunism in western Europe in those years.

Second characteristic that must be taken into account: since 1894-1895 the Russian working class never lost contact with its party. Its numerical entity can be deduced from Lenin's data on members:

1894-1895 - Several hundred workers

1906 - Around 33,000 members attend the Stockholm congress

1907 - 150,000-170,000 members

1913 - 33,000-50,000.

Lenin provides these figures in 1913, while arguing with Vera Zasulic, who claims that Russian social democracy is made up of trends of intellectuals. It is natural that this situation needs to be taken into account when dealing with organizational problems. It is Lenin himself who categorically states this in the preface to the aforementioned *Twelve Years* collection.

4. Against Localism, for Communist Centralization

The congress of 1898 created an underground organization and tried to start publishing an illegal newspaper, but the central leadership was almost immediately dispersed by the police, and the work could not continue. The organization was reduced to clubs, local groups without any structured link among them and without any continuity of work.

Lenin rejects the argument, which still found a broad appreciation among the Russian socialists, according to which the greatest need would have been to develop the network of local circles and to multiply and strengthen the local press.

The most urgent issue of the movement instead for him no longer consisted in the development of the old local and uncoordinated work, it was that, of *"uniting—of organization. This is a step for which a program is a necessity. The program must formulate our basic views; precisely establish our immediate political tasks; point out the immediate demands that must show the area of agitational activity; give unity to the agitational work, expand and deepen it, thus raising it from fragmentary partial agitation for petty, isolated demands to the status of agitation for the sum total of Social-Democratic demands"* (Lenin, Collected Works in 45 volumes, Lawrence and Wishart, London: IV, 230. In the rest of the text the mere mention of a volume and pages will refer to this work).

5. The revolution is not a matter of forms of organization

Even if, as we shall see, the organizational question was the main task of the moment, however, a vulgar fable must be debunked: that the particular form given to the Bolshevik party, apart from its doctrine and program, has made it an instrument capable in itself, with its discipline, of stirring up a revolution.

This does not detract from the importance of how the party organizes itself, and the history of the Bolshevik party, in the specific situation of Russia, shows this. Through questions of organization all forms of opportunism repeatedly try to penetrate into the party. Hence its tireless struggle for an organization well connected to the theoretical foundations of Marxism.

A period of dispersion and confusion begins, which Lenin describes both in *What is to be done?* and in the aforementioned preface. The characteristics of this period (1898-1903) are the following:

1) The workers are on the move;

2) Intellectual youth increasingly passes to Marxism and becomes infatuated with the workers' movement;

3) Any centralized organization, any continuous and unitary work is missing;

4) The workers' movement, the legal Marxist literature and revisionism take hold on young revolutionaries. It is the era of clubs: this is how Lenin describes it.

5) Terrorist and anarchist tendencies are revived as a reaction.

As the organization abroad of the RSDLP is the "Union of Russian Social democrats", of which is part Plechanov's "Emancipation of Labor Group". The publication of a central party organ, *"Rabociaia Gazieta"*, is attempted; Lenin writes a few articles for it, but it is never published. In Russia there are only local newspapers and other publications.

6. Against Economism – Economic Struggle and Political Struggle

Economism was born, that is, the tendency to overestimate the importance of the spontaneous economic struggle of the proletariat, and to underestimate its political tasks.

Who were the Economists, and what was their program, as summarized in the *Credo* of 1899, but already presented in an article of *Rabociaia Mysl* of October 1897? In the latter writing the Economists (who we would rightly call today, with very few differences, Workerists) state that the *"economic struggle is the way towards further victories"*; *"Let the workers fight for themselves, and not for future generations…"*; *"Workers for workers"*. The party, the perspectives of the revolution (not to mention Marxism and revolutionary theory), are not mentioned.

The consequence of economism is the theoretical justification of the system of local circles. Bernsteinism is closely linked to economism, which also devalues the tasks of the proletariat in the bourgeois revolution and supports the need for a "criticism" of the Marxist theory in the reformist sense. Economism permeates many Russian circles creating an anti-party, anti-organization, anti-theory, etc. mentality. Lenin immediately opposed it with a meeting of seventeen militants deported to Siberia, who spoke out for the condemnation of those positions. Lenin demolishes them in the *"A Protest by Russian Social-Democrats"*, written in 1899 on behalf of the exiled social-democratic community in Siberia:

"It is not true to say that the working class in the West did not take part in the struggle for political liberty and in political revolutions. The history of the Chartist movement and the revolutions of 1848 in France, Germany, and Austria prove the opposite. It is absolutely untrue to say that "Marxism was the theoretical expression of the prevailing practice: of the political struggle predominating over the economic." On the contrary, "Marxism" appeared at a time when non-political socialism prevailed (Owenism, "Fourierism," "true socialism") and the Communist Manifesto *took up the cudgels at once against non-political socialism. Even when Marxism came out fully armed with theory (*Capital*) and organized the celebrated International Working Men's Association, the political struggle was by no means the prevailing practice (narrow trade-unionism in England, anarchism and Proudhonism in the Romance countries). In Germany the great historic service performed by Lassalle was the transformation of the working class from an appendage of the liberal bourgeoisie into an independent political party. Marxism linked up the economic and the political struggle of the working class into a single inseparable whole; and the effort of the authors of the* Credo *to separate these forms of struggle is one of their most clumsy and deplorable departures from*

Marxism." "Similarly, there can be no suggestion of a "radical change in the practical activity" of the West-European workers parties, in spite of what the authors of the Credo *say: the tremendous importance of the economic struggle of the proletariat, and the necessity for such a struggle, were recognized by Marxism from the very outset. As early as the forties Marx and Engels conducted a polemic against the utopian socialists who denied the importance of this struggle."* (IV, 175-176).

7. Against "Free Criticism"

In 1900 the Social Democratic organization abroad split, a part of which passes over to economism and freedom of criticism. The "Union" publishes the "Rabocieie Dielo", which is imbued with economism and Bernsteinism, but tries to conceal it. It is for the reconstitution of the party's organizational unity on the theoretical basis of "freedom of criticism" and on the practical basis of "broad democracy" in the organization. Plechanov breaks away from the Union and founds the organization "Social Democrat".

The need for organizational unification is clearly felt, because all the work in Russia is falling apart ruined by localism, by approximation, by artisanal and generic methods.

Iskra and its circle take the field on the problem of the reconstitution of the party at the end of 1900. Among the Social Democrats there are the following positions:

1) The real economists, who do not even feel the need for the organization and devalue its importance; they are the theorizers of what exists in the present moment.

2) The tendency of *Raboceie Dielo*; shapeless trend that defends the legitimacy of revisionism and "freedom of criticism", on a theoretical level, a purely organizational unification guaranteed by internal democracy, on a practical level.

3) The *Iskra*; which wants to base the organization on the net clarification of theoretical, programmatic and tactical positions, and wants to break with economism.

The *Iskra* intends to reassert Marxist orthodoxy and make the periodical the ideological headquarters that acts as a link among all revolutionary Marxists; in its first issue of December 1900 its constant concern is disclosed: to infuse the proletarian masses with social-democratic ideas and conscience, organize a strong and disciplined party of full-time revolutionaries, and through them create solid links with the spontaneous workers' movement. This is to prevent workers from slipping into reformism and intelligentsia to remain at the superficial level of mere doctrinal disputes.

In June 1901, the representatives of the organizations in exile met in Geneva. The unity achieved in that conference proved to be short-lived and the *Iskra* consequently stiffened and became increasingly skeptical about the possibilities of achieving unification. In October of the same year, a new conference was held in Zurich which, after lively discussions, ended with the complete breakdown by the left. Immediately after *Iskra*, militants from the Social-Demokrat group and others join together in a new organization, the League of Russian Revolutionary Social Democracy. In their programmatic declaration they declare themselves proud to be called "sectarians".

8. *"What is to be done ?"* a milestone of Marxism

The most complete expression of the Iskrist campaign is *What is to be done?* in which Lenin poses all questions from a coherently Marxist point of view:

1) Theory, its importance and its invariance.

2) Function of the proletariat in the double revolution: necessity of the autonomous party and of the proletarian political struggle.

3) Relations between party and class, between tradeunionist politics and socialdemocratic politics, between spontaneity and conscience.

4) Finally, an organizational plan. Are needed:

a) a single political newspaper for all Russia.

b) a clandestine organization of professional revolutionaries closely anchored to principles, well delimited from the outside, uninterrupted over time and connected in space, surrounded by a whole series of legal and semi-legal organizations, specialized in practical work and strictly centralized.

c. a planned tactic, descending from the principles and that does not change overnight.

As concerns theory, Lenin is categorical, and he doesn't hesitate to call Engels to testify, by amply quoting him (V, 371-372), to demonstrate how the German workers themselves, at that very moment in the vanguard in Europe, had taken advantage of the theoretical conquests of the struggles and of the consequent theoretical elaborations that took place in France and England in the field of political and economic struggle.

The problem was represented by the defenders of the "freedom of criticism", whom Lenin defines *"freedom for an opportunist trend in Social-Democracy, freedom to convert Social-Democracy into a democratic party of reform, freedom to introduce bourgeois ideas and bourgeois elements into socialism."* (V, 355).

What is to be done? is a text of ours in all respects. *Iskra*'s organizational plan can be shared in all its smallest details.

9. From Circles to Party

We note that Lenin raises the question of the rigid delimitation of the organization of revolutionaries from other organizations, including workers'. He also raises the question of the maximum specialization in the field of practical action, but not in the work of theoretical study. We also note that Lenin raises the question of instruments, means really able to organize and not organizational or hierarchical formulas. Communal work for a communal newspaper; party organizations that are accustomed by the work itself to react simultaneously to events, up to the insurrection. The newspaper as a collective organizer.

The same themes are taken up again in the *Letter to a comrade,* immediately following *What is to be done? "It would perhaps be possible to get along without Rules".* We are already at organic centralism.

The II Congress meets in August 1903, which must proceed with the reunification of the party, on the basis of *Iskra*'s propositions. Everyone is now accepting the Iskrist program, but Lenin notes and shows that acceptance of a program in words is not enough if the organizational discipline of the party is not accepted. This statement has no ordinary, but rather historical and dialectical meaning even if it is perfectly acceptable to us. Think about it: there was economism until yesterday, there were circles until yesterday with their own vision, their own structure, their own tradition, there was and still is Bernsteinism. *Iskra* has hammered its propositions for 3 years and the situation of the material struggle has slowly forced all militants either to openly take sides with *Iskra* or to admit the plan of *Iskra* as the only valid one.

Lenin did not mean the same thing as others with the word "unification". The meaning he gave it was this: unity of the presently autonomous local circles of the Marxist movement in a party controlled by the center and ideologically homogeneous for all Russia. Unique discipline and ideological homogeneity: that was "unification". To reach it he was ready to reject compromises and let go all those who would not have accepted a centralized organization, all newspapers unwilling to merge into one national body, the Jewish Socialist Bund if it had not been ready to give up its autonomy, the Revisionists and the Economists and all those who were not ready to accept without discussion the "orthodox" Marxist program, which he, Plekhanov and the other editors of *Iskra* would have prepared for the next congress.

There were some who thought that the first requirement of the unborn party was a prolonged, full and free discussion of fundamental principles. But for Lenin, as for Plekhanov, all this had already been solved in Western Europe by the works of Marx and Engels and again by those of Kautsky and Plekhanov in their controversy still heated with Bernstein.

The congress is therefore convened, in view of the "acceptance" of the Iskrist plan. Well, gentlemen, words are not enough, facts are needed. And we iskrists put facts forth to you that show whether your acceptance is real or just words. To you who until yesterday were defending the legitimacy of what exists, let us put this touchstone: all circles must be dissolved, and all newspapers suppressed, there are no imperative mandates to the congress.

10. The Crucial First Paragraph

And the test bears fruit.

To you who until yesterday defended the organizations for the economic struggle and the party as the ideal superior instance, we propose a first paragraph of the statute that sounds like this: "A member of the party is not only the one who accepts the program and supports it to the extent of his forces, but he who also works in one of the party organizations. Are you really for the distinction between party and class? Prove it by accepting these conditions".

The discussion on the first paragraph is important because it raises the wider question of party organization. Lenin states: *"The definition given in my draft was: 'A member of the Russian Social-Democratic labor Party is one who accepts its program and who supports the Party both financially and by personal participation in one of the Party organizations.' In place of the words I have underlined, Martov proposed: 'work under the control and direction of one of the Party organizations.' My formulation was supported by Plekhanov, Martov's by the rest of the editorial board (Axelrod was their spokesman at the Congress). We argued that the concept of the Party member must be narrowed so as to separate those who worked from those who merely talked, to eliminate organizational chaos, to eliminate the monstrous and absurd possibility of there being organizations which consisted of Party members but which were not Party organizations, and so on. Martov stood for broadening the Party and spoke of a broad class movement needing a broad—i.e., diffuse— organization, and so forth. It is amusing to note that in defense of their views nearly all Martov's supporters cited What Is To Be Done?[4] Plekhanov hotly opposed Martov, pointing out that his Jauresist formulation would fling open the doors to the opportunists, who just longed for such a position of being inside the Party but outside its organization. 'Under the control and direction', I said, 'would in practice mean nothing more nor less than without any control or direction.'"* (VII, 27-28). Martov hoped for a mass party, but in doing so he opened the doors to all sorts of opportunists, made the party's limits indeterminate and vague. And this was a serious danger, as it was not easy to distinguish the boundary between the revolutionary and the idle chatterbox: Lenin says that a good third of the participants to the congress were schemers.

Why worry about those who don't want to or can't join one of the party organizations, Plekhanov wondered. *"Workers wishing to join the party will not be afraid to join one of its organizations. Discipline doesn't scare them. Intellectuals, completely imbued with bourgeois individualism, will fear entering. These bourgeois individualists are generally the representatives of all sorts of opportunism. We have to get them away from us. The project is a shield against their breaking into the party, and only for this reason should all enemies of opportunism vote for Lenin's proposal*"(Proceedings of the II congress, session of August 2 (#15); the minutes are from the website:https://www.marxists.org/history/internation al/socialdemocracy/rsdlp/1903/index.htm).

Trotsky speaks against Lenin's proposal, considering it ineffective. Lenin replies to him: *"[Trotsky] has failed to notice a basic question: does my formulation narrow or expand the concept of a Party member? If he had asked himself that question, he would easily have seen that my formulation narrows this concept, while Martov's expands it, for (to use Martov's own correct expression) what distinguishes his concept is its 'elasticity' And in the period of Party life that we are now passing through it is just this 'elasticity' that undoubtedly opens the door to all elements of confusion, vacillation, and opportunism."*

11. Organizational Steadfastness, Tactical Coherence, Purity of Principles

The unstable elements are harbingers of uncertainties, deviations, and little work. The danger can be great: *"The need to safeguard the Party's hard line and the purity of its principles has now become particularly urgent, for, with the restoration of its unity, the Party will recruit into its ranks a great many unstable elements, whose number will increase with the growth of the Party"* (VI, 499-500).

On the other hand, where is the danger of a rigorous delimitation of the party, through specific limits to the definition of social democrat? *"If hundreds and thousands of workers who were arrested for taking part in strikes and demonstrations did not prove to be members of Party organizations, it would only show that we have good organizations, and that we are fulfilling our task of keeping a more or less limited circle of leaders secret and of drawing the broadest possible masses into the movement."* But the party, a vanguard component of the working class, cannot be confused with the whole class, as Axelrod did. *"It would be better if ten who do work should not call themselves Party members (real workers don't hunt after titles!) than that one who only talks should have the right and opportunity to be a Party member." "The Central Committee will never be able to exercise real control over all who do the work but do not belong to organizations. It is our task to place actual control in the hands of the Central Committee. It is our task to safeguard the firmness, consistency, and purity of our Party. We must strive to raise the title and the significance of a Party member higher, higher, and still higher."* (VI, 500-502).

12. Professional revolutionaries

"Apparently Lenin seemed to distinguish between simple party militants and 'professional revolutionaries', whose small groups formed the

*backbone of the leadership. We have repeatedly
shown that this was the illegal network, not the
overlapping of a bureaucratic apparatus of paid
people on the party. Professional does not
necessarily mean salaried, but rather dedicated to
the struggle of the party for voluntary choice,
separated from any association for the defense of
collective interests, even if this remains the
deterministic basis for the very existence of the
party. The whole range of Marxist dialectics is in
this double relationship. The worker is
revolutionary for class interest, the communist is
revolutionary for the same purpose, but elevated
beyond the subjective interest.*" (Russia and
revolution in Marxist theory, 1955, Part 2, § 37).

"*The right wing of the Russian party wanted to
recruit the party members from professional or
factory groups of workers federated in the party; the
trade unions were called professional associations
by the Russians. For polemical purposes, Lenin
expresses the famous sentence that the party is
above all an organization of 'professional
revolutionaries.' We don't ask them: are you a wage
worker? In which profession? Mechanic,
boilermaker, carpenter? They can be factory
workers as well as students or even sons of
noblemen; their answer will be: 'Revolutionary',
this is my profession. Only Stalinist stupidity could
give to such sentence the meaning of revolutionary
by* trade, *of one salaried by the party. Such useless
formula: 'Should the functionaries be found among
the workers or elsewhere?' would not have made*

any progress, because it was about something completely different." (The Croaking about Praxis, Il Programma Comunista, n. 11/1953).

13. Knowledge and militancy – The "proletarian consciousness"

So for the Bolsheviks the revolutionary militant is he who accepts (and does not necessarily *know* or *understand* in detail) the program, and is willing to work under the orders of the party: abnegation qualities, willingness to fight, that any proletarian can have, even if illiterate. An acceptance of the program that can be based on the understanding of a few qualifying aspects, sometimes only of slogans, but which coincide with his deep aspirations, with his needs. An adhesion based more on passion than on intellect. Understanding will come over time, but never complete; on the other hand, total understanding of the doctrine can never be of the individual, but of the collective of the party, and is expressed in its press, in its theses, in its revolutionary tactics. *"... doctrinal knowledge is not an individual fact, even by the most cultured follower or leader, nor is it a condition for the mass in motion: it has as its subject its own organ, the party.*" (Russia and revolution, cit., § 32).

This concept is repeated in the Theses of 1952: *"The question of individual conscience is not the basis of the formation of the party: not only can't each proletarian be conscious, and least of all culturally master of the class doctrine, but not even an individual militant, and this guarantee is not even given by the leaders. It only exists in the organic unity of the party."* (Characteristic theses of the party, 1952).

"Beyond the influence of social democracy, there is no other conscious activity of the workers," says Lenin at the second congress; and we add: *"It is heavy, but it is so. So, the action of the proletarians is* spontaneous *in that it arises from economic determinants but does not have 'conscience' as a condition, neither in the individual nor in the class. The physical class struggle is an unconscious, spontaneous deed. The class reaches its conscience only when the revolutionary party has formed within it, which possesses the theoretical conscience based on the real class relationship, characteristic of all proletarians. These, however, will never be able to possess its true knowledge - that is, theory - neither as individuals, nor as a whole, nor as a majority, as long as the proletariat is subject to bourgeois education and culture, that is, to the bourgeois fabrication of its ideology and, in clear terms, until the proletariat wins, and...ceases to exist. So, in exact terms, proletarian consciousness will never be. There is doctrine, communist knowledge, and this is in the party of the proletariat, not in the class."* (Ibid., § 39).

14. Autonomy, Dmocracy, Open Criticism

Bolsheviks and Mensheviks form the two organized fractions of the RSDLP from 1903 to 1906.

The congress was to be an arena of struggle, and it really was. As the Bolsheviks set their conditions, there were opposed positions. And where necessarily? In the organizational question. All those who had previously been opponents of *Iskra* theoretically, programmatically and tactically, now shouted against centralism and discipline, were for the autonomy and democracy of the organization; they accused the revolutionary wing of bureaucratism, of imposing a "state of siege". But all Lenin's bureaucratism is to pose a state of siege on opportunist positions. All the alleged "manoeuvrism" of Lenin, who on the contrary never abandons sincere and fraternal, non-political, behaviors with all comrades, including the opposers.

He had been the champion of the involvement of the party in economic struggles of the working class in the 1895-1897 period; still he had to destroy the economists' positions in the years preceding the second congress. Now it was the moment to defend bureaucratism, to dispel the greed for freedom of criticism, of autonomy within the party: centralism as a primary necessity. This was not understood then by Trotsky and Luxemburg.

All this Lenin narrates in the 1904 work *One step forward, two steps back*, where he notes the split of social democracy into two wings as a positive fact. The division of the party into two opposed factions, Lenin notes, is characteristic of all the parties of the Second International. The division has roots in the social situation of the proletariat. The same is confirmed after the IV Congress of 1906 (X, 422). The opportunist current (legal Marxism, economism, Menshevism) represents the influence of the petty bourgeoisie on the proletariat. Here's how Lenin poses the question: *"In all capitalist countries the proletariat is inevitably connected by a thousand transitional links with its neighbor on the right, the petty bourgeoisie. In all workers' parties there inevitably emerges a more or less clearly delineated Right-wing which, in its views, tactics, and organizational 'line', reflects the opportunist tendencies of the petty bourgeoisie"* (XIII, 113).

The attitude that the Bolsheviks held in the years up to 1917, of tolerance within the party of unorthodox or uncertain currents, varies in view of the expectation of maturation in a Marxist, radical direction after experiences of the movement; otherwise a clear-cut and intransigent differentiation and separation, whenever scarce clarity and uncertainties in tactics can be detrimental for the outcome of the struggle. Choices in countries with a scarce and immature proletariat, like Russia at the time, are legitimate. Lenin will be much more determined after the outbreak of the war, and after the foundation of the Third International, even if not enough for us when measures were to be applied to the parties of the West.

15. Executive Discipline is Unavoidable

After the Congress, a part of the *Iskra* group that had refused to dissolve, gathering all the dissatisfied around it and sabotaged the normal course of all-party work. The last part of the booklet and the epithet of "anarchism of the 'noble' gentleman, or aristocratic anarchism" are dedicated to this attitude that did not recognize the decisions of the Congress and the submission of the minority to the majority. The formal rules that still governed the confrontation of opinions within the party provided - according to "democratic centralism" - for the submission of the minority, which was, however, guaranteed the possibility of freely expressing and arguing its opinions in front of the whole party. This discussion among comrades of the same party was regulated by precise forms and customs, always careful to avoid lacerations and damage to the organization. The Party is the general staff of an army at war and under the fire of the enemy: it is excluded that its unity of action, its executive discipline, will be broken. That "ideal struggle", the word is Lenin's, between a "majority" and a "minority", in "democratic" forms, has had its place in the life of the Party, of course, as long as it has been inevitable, due to historical immaturity, the confrontation between opposite directions and conceptions. This must never get to breaking the unity of action, the executive discipline. For Lenin, and for us, belonging to the party means to work with, and for, the party: "…this very fact of refusing to work together is nothing but a split" (VII, 165).

This "ideal struggle" in the RSDLP remained until 1906, with several attempts made by the Bolsheviks to bring the Mensheviks back to work. Of course, practical work in Russia was greatly affected by this situation and fell almost entirely on the Bolsheviks.

In May 1905, on the initiative of the Bolshevik committees, the III Congress was held in London, in which the tactics for the next revolution were defined. The Mensheviks simultaneously convene a conference in Geneva, where they adopt completely opposite tactical resolutions. In *Two Tactics of Social Democracy*, written in July 1905, Lenin still proposes the unification of tactics as the basis for the future unification of the party. The thesis is still that "the revolution instructs", that is, it is still possible that the Mensheviks, as a current having a basis in the workers' movement, abandon their propositions, driven by the facts. The booklet is clearly in tune for this purpose.

From October to December 1905 there were great revolutionary events. Under the pressure of these and their effective working base, the Mensheviks support the proletariat even if in an uncertain and hesitant manner. The possibility of an organizational reunification arises.

The two fractions go to the congress (the fourth, April 1906). The congress is in the majority for Mensheviks. Lenin explains the conditions of unification, but it is significant that he reaffirms the importance of the theory: *"In view of the coming formidable, decisive events in the people's struggle, it is all the more essential to attain the practical unity of the class-conscious proletariat of the whole of Russia, and of all her nationalities. In a revolutionary epoch like the present, all theoretical errors and tactical deviations of the Party are most ruthlessly criticized by experience itself, which enlightens and educates the working class with unprecedented rapidity. At such a time, the duty of every Social-Democrat is to strive to ensure that the ideological struggle within the Party on questions of theory and tactics is conducted as openly, widely, and freely as possible, but that on no account does it disturb or hamper the unity of revolutionary action of the Social-Democratic proletariat."* (X, 310-311).

This is important, because it poses the question of discipline in the situation where the revolutionary wing is in the minority, although defending the clearest and unambiguous distinction between the two wings, and allowing ample space for freedom of internal criticism, etc. *"The Central Committee's resolution is essentially wrong and* runs counter to the Party Rules. *The principle of democratic centralism and autonomy for local Party organizations implies universal and full* freedom to

criticize, *so long as this does not disturb the unity of
a definite action; it rules out* all *criticism which
disrupts or makes difficult the* unity *of an action
decided on by the Party*" (X, 443).

At the same Congress, Lenin makes an *a-
posteriori* theoretical victory: the famous paragraph
1, which in the 2nd Congress had been included in
the party program in the Menshevik formulation, is
adopted in Lenin's wording.

In this period (the first part of 1906) the
Bolsheviks are for the boycott of the Duma (a
theoretical boycott though, because Witte's Duma
was never convened, and a reaction period
followed). The Mensheviks instead proposed
support for a Cadet minister; Lenin then appeals to
the right of party organizations and party
proletarians to discuss Central Committee decisions,
especially if they contradict Congress resolutions. In
short, in today's language, the Center has no right to
act or even theorize in contradiction with the party's
program.

16. The Alligations of "Leninist Creativity"

Lenin's *What is to be done?* is, as we all know, a
fundamental text for us left-wing revolutionary
Marxists, communist heirs of the Communist Left
(also called Italian Left), but nevertheless connected
to Lenin's Marxism. We acknowledge his theoretical
work in full, for it is grounded on the same

foundations on which the Left had grown; and the Left had achieved the same theoretical conclusions even before getting to know Lenin's works, which in the most part will only reach Italy several years after their publication in Russia (the first edition of *What is to be done?* in Italian was published in 1946, although in other languages the text was already known in the first post-war period by the Italian communists).

Nevertheless the need remains to demonstrate a continuity, often up to an identity of positions, between us and the Bolsheviks, to show to those who, by figuring a sort of Lenin's theoretical creativity, describe his doctrine as a novelty in the Marxist landscape, to be associated with the many novelties that have plagued the revolutionary movement of the proletariat over the decades.

That of the innovations, of the tactical and theoretical inventions, of the shrewd maneuvering of Lenin, is a legend that does not stand up to an honest reading of his writings, which we will try to do here, at least in relation to a key period of the formation of the RSDLP (Russian Social Democratic labor Party), the period around the second party congress (1901-1904).

That of falsification of Lenin's thought - which obviously was nothing more than consequent Marxism, always better defined and, as we say, "sculpted" - is a work that has allowed hordes of intellectuals orbiting in the areas more or less "left" of the workers' movement to earn from the bourgeoisie a definitely deserved salary, given the damage caused to the same movement. In Italy the most important sphere for this purpose of the left was, as long as it existed, that of the Italian Communist Party, to which many historians, philosophers, sociologists, etc., made reference; these, for over 50 years, have given their best to refute Marxism by pretending to exalt it. The technique is always the same: we start by recognizing the historical significance of given theses and positions, to then insert almost in passing a poisonous word that effectively nullifies their revolutionary force. It is the technique of Stalinism, which not by chance coined the disgraceful term of "Leninism". Hot years, woe to say the wrong of Lenin and his writings openly; therefore, a difficult job, requiring skilled craftsmen, prestigious intellectuals, and many made themselves available.

For Lenin, as for us, the theory of revolution was born in a single block from the Manifesto of 1848, and is then defined, clarified, and deepened in the subsequent writings of Marx and Engels, and also in those of Lenin, never in contradiction with those of the two great maestros; on the contrary, by citing them often, whenever he had to defend assumptions hard to accept by the less equipped comrades.

For them instead the elaboration process that should take place in the party is to be understood not in our sense and in Lenin's sense of sculpting, but rather of continuous revision, adaptation to the allegedly changing conditions in which the labor movement would find itself. For them when Lenin wrote in 1899 that *"We think that an* independent *elaboration of Marx's theory is especially essential for Russian socialists"* (IV, 213), he meant a development not only of tactics, but also of revolutionary theory, a "concrete analysis of the concrete situation"; pity that the article from which the citation is taken, *"Our program"*, was hurled precisely at the innovators Bernstein-style (far more to the left, anyway, than the PCI leaders 1950s-70s), while he defends himself, as we have to do all the time, from accusations of dogmatism; in that same article our Vladimir reminds that *"Marx's theory … has only laid the foundation stone of the science which socialists* must *develop in all directions"*. This is the meaning of the *"independent elaboration"* of which Lenin speaks, and not that of the dismantling of Marxism, including cornerstones and foundations.

Other Stalinists have evoked an elusive *"new Marxist theory of revolution"* by Lenin. In this they are in good company, with Trotskyists: Mandel, for example, who writes of an alleged *"original development"* of the Marxist theory by Lenin, or others of the "far" left, for whom no parts of Marxism *"can be dogmatically fixed, they require a continual re-elaboration and development"*, and a hundred others, of greater or lesser political caliber, all however eager to find substantial innovations in what they call "Leninism", to legitimize their discoveries, their innovations, their ideological filth. The technique of extrapolating sentences from the context and then using them to affirm the opposite of what the original work defends goes back to Stalin, but many students have gone beyond the master in the technique of falsification, and have filled millions of pages of anti-communist and anti-proletarian trash. In reaffirming the foundations of Marxism in Lenin we are therefore forced to employ not very brief quotations, and to place them in the true historical and political context in which the texts of Lenin himself were expressed.

17. No "New Type Party"

But what was the Party for our two founding masters? It is worth remembering to the Philistines who fill their mouths with Marx and Engels' at every turn, what the working-class party was for them, and from what fountains Lenin drank deep in his work to build the revolutionary party.

The Manifesto reads:

"Now and then the workers are victorious, but only for a time. The real fruit of their battles lies, not in the immediate result, but in the ever-expanding union of the workers."

"*This organization of proletarians into a class,* and consequently into a political party, *is continually being upset again by the competition between the workers themselves. But it ever rises up again, stronger, firmer, mightier.*" (M-E, Collected Works, VI 494-495).

"*The Communists are distinguished from the other working-class parties by this only: In the national struggles of the proletarians of the different countries, they point out and bring to the front the*

*common interests of the entire proletariat,
independently of all nationality"*

*"The Communists, therefore, are on the one
hand, practically, the most advanced and resolute
section of the working-class parties of every
country, that section which pushes forward all
others; on the other hand, theoretically, they have
over the great mass of the proletariat the advantage
of clearly understanding the line of march, the
conditions, and the ultimate general results of the
proletarian movement. The immediate aim of the
Communists is the same as that of all other
proletarian parties: formation of the proletariat into
a class, overthrow of the bourgeois supremacy,
conquest of political power by the proletariat. The
theoretical conclusions of the Communists are in no
way based on ideas or principles that have been
invented, or discovered, by this or that would-be
universal reformer. They merely express, in general
terms, actual relations springing from an existing
class struggle, from a historical movement going on
under our very eyes. (M-E, VI, 498-499).*

*"In its struggle against the collective power of
the propertied classes, the working class cannot act
as a class except by constituting itself into a
political party, distinct from, and opposed to all old
parties formed by the propertied classes. This
constitution of the working class into a political
party is indispensable in order to insure the triumph
of the social revolution, and of its ultimate end, the
abolition of classes." (M-E, XXIII, 243).*

"We agree that the proletariat cannot conquer political power, the only way to enter the new society, without a violent revolution. In order for the proletariat to be strong enough to win on the decisive day it is necessary - and this Marx and I have supported it since 1847 - that a specific party be formed, separate from all the others and opposed to them, a class party conscious of self." "Like all other parties, the proletariat learns first of all from the consequences of its mistakes, and nobody can spare them these mistakes altogether." (Engels to Trier, 18 December 1889).

"Our views as to the points of difference between a future, non-capitalistic society and that of today, are strict conclusions from existing historical facts and developments, and of no value – theoretical or practical – unless presented in connection with these facts and developments." (M-E, XLVII, 392).

"…every reverse suffered was a necessary consequence of mistaken theoretical views in the original program." (M-E, XLVII, 541).

These few and meager quotations, which certainly do not replace the immense theoretical corpus that we inherited from our teachers, are however sufficient to establish firm points to understand the nature and role of the proletarian party, and to beat in advance the criticisms that were then moved to Lenin, and subsequently also to us:

1) the need of the party to be able to win in the final struggle with the opposing classes, a

struggle that will necessarily and inevitably be violent;

2) the class is such only if organized in the party, otherwise it exists only for statistics, but not for itself;

3) class consciousness resides only in the party, and not in individuals, proletarians or not;

4) the theory of revolution is scientific, and cannot ignore past, present and future; it is embodied in the program, which can be continuously improved in the light of errors and experiences, but precisely because scientific cannot be contradicted by new events.

Lenin's greatness did not therefore consist in the elaboration of a new type of party, as the "Leninists" would have us believe, thus introducing the usual asset of everything that changes, the need for discoveries, new ways, "original" elaborations. Lenin drew from his profound knowledge of Marxist science the project of a party that was, from an organizational point of view, of course, but in the end also theoretically, capable of winning the clash with capitalism, incumbent also in Russia, and with Tsarism. Its formula, born for the birth of a true revolutionary Marxist party suited to the conditions of Russia, is in its main outline equally valid for all the parties that were at that time socialist, then communist. It is in the light of the foregoing that it is necessary to evaluate what Lenin defends in his writings from the birth period of the Russian Social

Democratic labor Party, which are the main object of this work.

18. Dogmatic Marxism Vs. Revisionism

Lenin starts off by reminding the questions posed in *Where To Begin: "the character and main content of our political agitation; our organizational tasks; and the plan for building, simultaneously and from various sides, a militant, all-Russia organization"* (V, 349).

The discussion will certainly focus on the criticism of economism but will give the opportunity to shed light on many other central issues of the movement.

The first chapter is entitled *Dogmatism and "Freedom of Criticism"*. Lenin is quick to clarify the point that is most important to him, that of the so-called "dogmatic Marxism", of which he admits to being a messenger, internationally threatened by the new wave of "critics", the famous revisionism of Bernstein and others. In this fundamental chapter Lenin denounces revisionism, and in general the attempt to erase the scientific basis of socialism; with "new" arguments one gets to deny or question all the cornerstones of Marxism, including the theory of class struggle. For him, this is only a new variety of opportunism, dressed up as an expression of freedom, freedom of criticism: " *'Freedom' is a grand word, but under the banner of freedom for industry the most predatory wars were waged, under the banner of freedom of labor, the working people were robbed. The modern use of the term 'freedom of criticism' contains the same inherent falsehood."* (V, 355)

Since then we know how many times this word, which does not belong to the vocabulary of the revolution in the sense meant by the bourgeois, has been used to perpetrate the most atrocious crimes, including wars that have cost tens of millions of lives. No freedom has arisen, but rather the enslavement of entire continents to the interests of international capital.

19. "A Compact Group"

Lenin concludes the chapter with a period that is among the most famous of his literature: *"We are marching in a compact group along a precipitous and difficult path, firmly holding each other by the hand. We are surrounded on all sides by enemies, and we have to advance almost constantly under their fire. We have combined, by a freely adopted decision, for the purpose of fighting the enemy, and not of retreating into the neighboring swamp, the inhabitants of which, from the very outset, have reproached us with having separated ourselves into an exclusive group and with having chosen the path of struggle instead of the path of conciliation. And now some among us begin to cry out: Let us go into the swamp! And when we begin to shame them, they retort: What backward people you are! Are you not ashamed to deny us the liberty to invite you to take a better road! Oh, yes, gentlemen! You are free not only to invite us, but to go yourselves wherever you will, even into the swamp. In fact, we think that the swamp is your proper place, and we are prepared to render you every assistance to get there. Only let go of our hands, don't clutch at us and don't besmirch the grand word freedom, for we too are "free" to go where we please, free to fight not only against the swamp, but also against those who are turning towards the swamp!"* (Ibid.).

Of course, the pamphlet, and the controversy, mainly concern the representatives of opportunism present in the Russian socialist movement; who assert that *"For a durable unity, there must be freedom of criticism"*, *"against the ossification of thought"*. Lenin recalls that Engels himself, on several occasions, inveighed against those who wanted to interpret the theory of socialism in the most imaginative, and above all unscientific, ways; and that the defenders of critical freedom in Russia are neither free nor critical of Bernsteinism.

Opportunism is one of the major dangers for the party: an enemy of theory, when it devotes itself to it, it does so to bend it to its purposes, often dressed up as "common sense"; which are always those of curbing revolutionary work to favor contingent, irrelevant, and often bogus purposes. For the opportunists, the subject is the ordinary worker, for whom they are inclined to indulge all his prejudices, to "religiously contemplate his backside", to use Plekhanov's expression. If the worker is mainly concerned with internal issues in the factory, the opportunist becomes a "pure unionist": "the masses are always right".

Having explained in what terms we can and must be allied with bourgeois democratic movements (that is, maintaining the freedom to reveal to the working class that its interests and those of the bourgeoisie are opposed), the text goes on to explain how to battle opportunism. *"First, they should have made efforts to resume the theoretical work that had barely begun in the period of legal Marxism and that fell anew on the shoulders of the comrades working underground. Without such work the successful growth of the movement was impossible."* (V, 365), *"before we can unite, and in order that we may unite, we must first of all draw firm and definite lines of demarcation"* (V, 367). Therefore, it's nice to get together, but only if you share the essential cornerstones of Marxism; the fetish of the union as an end in itself must instead be banned.

A short chapter follows, whose title is sufficient to underline its importance, *"Engels On the Importance of the Theoretical Struggle"*. The economists quote, against the "dogmatics", a sentence of Marx: *"Every step of real movement is more important than a dozen programs"*. But Lenin is quick to throw back at them the attempt to diminish the importance of theory, quoting Marx, from the same document: *"To repeat these words in a period of theoretical disorder is like wishing mourners at a funeral many happy returns of the day. Moreover, these words of Marx are taken from his letter on the Gotha program, in which he sharply condemns eclecticism in the formulation of principles. If you must unite, Marx wrote to the party leaders, then enter into agreements to satisfy the practical aims of the movement, but do not allow any bargaining over principles, do not make theoretical "concessions"* (V, 369).

Lenin quotes a long passage from Engels about the importance of theory, and adds: *"Without revolutionary theory there can be no revolutionary movement"* ...*"the role of vanguard fighter can be fulfilled only by a party that is guided by the most advanced theory."* (V, 369-370). And which is this most advanced theory? This was already quite clear for Lenin as back as in 1899: *"Only the theory of revolutionary Marxism can be the banner of the class movement of the workers, and Russian Social-Democracy must concern itself with the further development and implementation of this theory and must safeguard it against the distortions and vulgarizations to which 'fashionable theories' are so often subjected"* (IV, 180). Lenin will remind it in clear words in 1920's *Left wing communism*: *"... Bolshevism arose in 1903 on a very firm foundation of Marxist theory....Bolshevism, which had arisen on this granite foundation of theory."* (XXXI, 25-26)

"If there was no proletarian utopianism in Russia, it is because, when the movement developed up to the preconditions for a party, the theory of this party was already done internationally, and came

from outside. (...) The party was right at 'importing' the already available instrument and weapon which is party theory. There is nothing in this of idealism. Marxism could not be formed, the discoveries that constitute it could not be reached, before the bourgeois mode of production had spread and the proletarian class had formed within it, in large and developed national societies; but, once formed, it is valid for the zones, the fields, which arrive late, and it is suitable to establish what will be the process that awaits them and that develops in the same way" (Russia and Revolution cit., Part 2, § 32; Programma Comunista n. 7, 1955).

In essence, Lenin starts from the long quotation from Engels to reaffirm the primacy of theory and program in the indissoluble entwining of all the fundamental aspects of the party's struggle: theoretical, political, and practical-economic.

Lenin is always very explicit in referring to the founders of modern socialism, in the years preceding the Congress: in 1899 (*Our program*) he writes: "*It* [Marxist theory] *made clear the real task of a revolutionary socialist party: not to draw up plans for refashioning society, not to preach to the capitalists and their hangers-on about improving the lot of the workers, not to hatch conspiracies,* but to organize the class struggle of the proletariat and to lead this struggle, the ultimate aim of which is the conquest of political power by the proletariat and the organization of a socialist society." (IV, 210-211). And to those who accuse him to overlook the economic struggle he replies: "*All Social-*

Democrats are agreed that it is necessary to organize the economic struggle of the working class, that it is necessary to carry on agitation among the workers on this basis, i.e., to help the workers in their day-to-day struggle against the employers, to draw their attention to every form and every case of oppression and in this way to make clear to them the necessity for combination. But to forget the political struggle for the economic would mean to depart from the basic principle of international Social-Democracy, it would mean to forget what the entire history of the labor movement teaches us." (IV, 212).

The following year he again feels the need to affirm his Marxist faith, in *Declaration of the editorial board of Iskra:* *"Before we can unite, and in order that we may unite, we must first of all draw firm and definite lines of demarcation. Otherwise, our unity will be purely fictitious, it will conceal the prevailing confusion and binder its radical elimination. It is understandable, therefore, that we do not intend to make our publication a mere storehouse of various views. On the contrary, we shall conduct it in the spirit of a strictly defined tendency. This tendency can be expressed by the word Marxism, and there is hardly need to add that we stand for the consistent development of the ideas of Marx and Engels and emphatically reject the equivocating, vague, and opportunist "corrections" for which Eduard Bernstein, P. Struve, and many others have set the fashion."* (IV, 354-355).

Therefore, in all his literature, Lenin never hesitates to draw liberally on Marx and Engels in support of the positions he defends inside and outside the party, and this not only in the birth stage of the organization, but throughout all his life, just read "*The State and Revolution*". Since the Samara period he used to say that he had to "*consult with Marx*" (the expression is his, quoted by Trotsky: "*The young Lenin*") when some critical argument was presented. Another testimony is from Krisov (*Lénine tel qu'il fut*, 1958): "*In general, the debates did not last long, because the issues had been studied previously. But if, nevertheless, a discussion broke out, Lenin did not impose his point of view, tried to weigh all the pros and cons, and sometimes declared: "We must postpone the decision to the next meeting to ask for Marx's opinion*".

Then as today the communists are reproached for living on old things, for not being able to renew themselves, for not paying attention to the new. In *"Some Reflections on the Letter from "7 Ts. 6 F."* (VI, 289, 292) Lenin writes: *"This is old stuff!" you wail. Yes. All parties that have* good *popular literature have been distributing* old stuff *for decades....And the* only *popular literature that is* good, *the* only *popular literature that is* suitable *is that which can serve* for decades...*And all you have is just one* Iskra; *after all, it gets monotonous! Thirty-one issues and all* Iskra, *while with the captivating people every two issues of one title (of trash) are immediately followed by three issues of another title (of trash). Now, this is energy, this is jolly, this is new!"* (VI, 289, 292). This is not a novelty for us who, today, remain jealously attached to "hitting old nails".

20. Sectarianism

Nor is it a novelty to dedicate our attacks and our criticism more to our "neighbors", and alleged "kindred" than to the declared enemies of the working class, from which the proletariat does not need to be helped to defend itself; in this we find an illustrious precedent in a letter from Marx to Kinkel (April 1850): "*Our task is unreserved criticism, more towards the supposed friends than the declared enemies; and, affirming our position, we gladly give up cheap democratic popularity.*" Are we the only ones to perceive in Marx a badly disguised contempt for democracy? On this our verbally transmitted tradition states: the closest to us are the worst.

This attitude of ours, which has also been demonstrated was of the great Lenin, has often earned us the title considered offensive of "sectarians". Well, it is a title that we do not reject, if on the opposite is the situationist, the opportunist, the one who seeks new ways, not so much for the sake of the revolution, as for exalting his ego, to be able to say that he gave a "contribution", if not to perpetrate the most miserable of betrayals. Thus, we treated the subject in 1959:

"Well known is the flavor that every lousy petty-bourgeois spirit gives to the objections and criticisms of our research to return to the original construction of Marxism. We would take, according to those kobolds, Marx's writing as a revealed verb to which we must blindly believe, we would follow it as a dogma that it is not permissible to discuss but to accept a priori. We would renounce the precious light of free individual criticism of our intellect and of those who follow us. We would deny that the unfolding of historical facts for over a century has been able to deny or at least modify those positions deduced using only the data of human history, prior to that period around 1850.

Well, fools born of degenerate bourgeois culture, this is precisely what we claim and propose! And we have the right to do so because our discovery, the first use of the formidable key that solved the antitheses and enigmas that weighed on humanity, already contained the scientific and critical conquest according to which your claims are empty and inconsistent lies" (The Economic and Social Structure of Russia Today, Programma Comunista n. 18, 1959).

On the other hand, how can Lenin himself not be accused of sectarianism (as the economists actually did in 1902), if with all his alleged maneuvering (always invoked by the lowlife who aspires to place the miserable himself on some page of history) he never hesitated to cut, to condemn, even to mock all those who pretended to adulterate the fundamental tables of Marxism? An anecdote of Ljiudvinskaja (in "Lénine tel qu'il fut", 1958) tells: "*In Paris, Lenin directed all our activity ... Lenin's harshness and intransigence against opportunists troubled some comrades. One of them said to Lenin:* "Why should we expel everyone from the section? With whom will we work? "*Lenin replied with a smile*: "It matters little if we are not very numerous today, because, on the other hand, we will be united in our action, and the conscious workers will support us, since we are on the right path.""

21. Where Does Consciousness Come From?

The next chapter, *The Spontaneity of the Masses and the Consciousness of the Social-Democrats* does not abandon the theme of the importance of theory. Where is the consciousness? Can the workers acquire it by virtue of their struggle experiences? History has shown us that this is not so, the socialist revolutionary consciousness can reach the proletarians only from the outside, outside the economic struggles, and Lenin strongly reaffirms this, in this confirmed by our great teachers: "*The ideas of the ruling class are the dominant ideas in every age; that is, the class which is the dominant material power of society is at the same time its dominant spiritual power. The class that disposes of the means of material production thus has at the*

*same time the means of intellectual production, so
that as a whole the ideas of those who lack the
means of intellectual production are subject to
it*"(M-E, V, 44). Hence: "[for the production of the
communist conscience]... *revolution is not necessary
only because the ruling class cannot be brought
down in any other way, but also because the class
that overthrows it can only succeed in a revolution
to rinse off all the old filth and to become capable of
founding society on new foundations*" (M-E, V, 38).

The doctrine of socialism derives from the
acquisitions of science, history, economics,
philosophy, which are the prerogative of the
possessing classes, which produce intellectuals. The
proletarians can arrive at a trade unionist
consciousness, that is, understand that they must
organize themselves into unions, that they must
conduct struggles in a certain way, that they can and
must make requests to the government for better
legislation, and perhaps organize themselves in this
sense, but they have not the tools to proceed further.

Lenin does not underestimate the importance of
spontaneity, on the contrary. He writes "*There is
spontaneity and spontaneity. [Compared with the
struggles of earlier years, also of the luddist type...]
the strikes of the nineties might even be described as
"conscious", to such an extent do they mark the
progress which the working-class movement made
in that period. This shows that the "spontaneous
element", in essence, represents nothing more nor
less than consciousness in an embryonic form.*" (V,
375).

But to expect more from spontaneous struggles is a submission to spontaneity, which has the sole consequence of reinforcing bourgeois influence on the class, and this is the consequence of spontaneists, not only the economists of the Russian polemic of the time, but also the anarchists, and generally those who disdain theory in favor of the worship of blue overalls. There is no middle ground: *"Since there can be no talk of an independent ideology formulated by the working masses themselves in the process of their movement, the only choice is — either bourgeois or socialist ideology."* (V, 384). Therefore *"…all worship of the spontaneity of the working class movement, all belittling of the role of "the conscious element", of the role of Social-Democracy, means, quite independently of whether he who belittles that role desires it or not*, a strengthening of the influence of bourgeois ideology upon the workers. " (V, 382-383). "

22. Workers in the Party

In a note, however, it is clarified, to disprove easy and dishonest criticisms of this lapidary thesis, that workers are not excluded from the study and sculpting of party doctrine, as well as from positions of responsibility in the party itself (and there are many examples of this), but these are workers who operate as communists in the party, not as workers; as humans who have risen to the revolutionary Marxist conscience, and have erased from their minds the place in which the bourgeois exploitation regime has locked them up. This regardless of the acquired cultural level, whether or not they became "intellectuals". The party does not require academic qualifications, which on the contrary push it to greater caution in accepting memberships, the party asks for the determination to work for the revolution, with the tools one has. The worker who enters the party ceases to be a worker, he becomes a militant communist, thus wrenching *"from his heart and his mind the classification under which he has been inscribed in the registry of this putrefying society"* (Considerations on the organic activity…, #11, 1965).

"The school of the proletarians will be the victorious revolution, which for now asks them for their armed hands, but cannot ask them for a political degree; even those who are party members are not asked a "culture examination". Since the struggles in the Second International the Left has mocked the thesis of the "cultured" party " (The theory of the primary function of the political party, only guardian and salvation of the historical energy of the proletariat), Programma Comunista no. 21-22, 1958).

23. The Mystique of Joining the Communists

We have already seen that other characteristics are required for joining the party other than

"Marxist" culture and individual knowledge of our doctrine; skills are required that Lenin called of courage, self-denial, heroism, spirit of sacrifice; it is in order to verify these qualities that discrimination is made between the sympathizer or candidate and the militant, the active soldier of the revolutionary army; certainly not because the sympathizer does not "know" yet, while the militant has consciousness. If this were not the case, the whole Marxist conception would fall, because the Communist Party is that body which must, in the moments of revolutionary recovery, organize millions of men, who will have neither the time nor the need to take courses in Marxism, even accelerate, and they will adhere to the party not because they know, but because they feel "*instinctively and spontaneously and without the slightest course of study that can mimic school qualifications*". And also because they are capable of dreaming, like the "cold organizer", the "rational" Lenin hopes in the same *What is to be done?* (V, 510). So joining responds first of all to a push that goes beyond rationality, total understanding, cold reasoning: a choice that we, distant pupils of Lenin, have not hesitated to call also mystical.

"The problem of knowledge that tormented the many currents of thought over the centuries is solved for us, as future universal science today has access to a party, which alone gives its name to the class that anticipates tomorrow. Just as the party is still halfway between the fiction of the individual and the marvelous "human" conquest of universality, so in history the ideological cement

*that distinguishes it lies beyond the ancient errors
that poured out the amount of truth for which they
arose and had to fall; it leads with a system of
principles that can still be called a mystique, the last
of the mystiques, whereby many will struggle and
fall not only in the supreme sacrifice of life, also will
fall the joy of checking everything before believing,
a joy that will only be achieved after the victory; the
surviving generation will be given this gift by the
last one that had the war-winning mission, in war of
humans against men.*" (The Economic and Social
Structure of Russia Today, Programma Comunista n.
18, 1959).

An anecdote from 1905 is interesting, when
Lenin, faced with the question of whether a priest -
however a non-Marxist - can be admitted to the
Social Democratic Party, responds positively,
placing the acceptance of the party's political
program as a condition for joining the party, even
when this is not accompanied by adherence to the
method-conception that the program underlies. "…a
political organization cannot put its members
through an examination to see if there is no
contradiction between their views and the Party
program." (XV, 408). Therefore belonging to the
party is verified in the course of party activity, not in
an impossible examination of the level of
consciousness.

24. Control of Bourgeois Ideology and the Law of Minimum Effort

Returning to the theme of the dominant culture, it is interesting in this regard a further passage of *What is to be done?: "But why, the reader will ask, does the spontaneous movement, the movement along the line of least resistance, lead to the domination of bourgeois ideology? For the simple reason that bourgeois ideology is far older in origin than socialist ideology, that it is more fully developed, and that it has at its disposal immeasurably more means of dissemination."* (V, 386).

At this point we can't avoid recalling an unwritten rule which is being passed down within the party of the Left since its beginnings: the correct path to have the correct results in our theoretical work is not that of minimum effort, but rather the longest one, that which requires most work; we do not adopt the bourgeois method, of maximum profit with minimum investment,; we are not in a hurry, we are not looking for the result at all costs.

"A fundamental feature of the phenomenon that Lenin named, branding it with a red-hot iron, with a term that is also in Marx and Engels, opportunism, is a preference for a shorter, more comfortable and less arduous way, to the longer, uncomfortable one fraught with difficulties; on which alone the matching of the assertion of our principles and

programs, i.e. of our supreme purposes, with the development of the immediate and direct practical action, in the real current situation, may take place." (Supplementary theses on the historical task, the action and the structure of the world communist party, #5, Programma Comunista n. 7, 1966).

Now it is worthwhile to quote a curious sentence, from a 1902 writing for internal circulation (VI, 70): *"If the Lord God has chosen to punish us for our sins by obliging us to come out with a "mongrel" draft, we should at least do every thing in our power to reduce the unhappy consequences. Therefore, those who are above all guided by a desire to "get through with it as quickly as possible" are quite wrong. It may be taken for granted that now, given such a constellation, nothing but evil will come of haste, and our editorial draft will be unsatisfactory. It is not absolutely necessary to publish it in No. 4 of Zarya: we can publish it in No. 5 .... If we do this, a delay of a month or so will do no harm at all to the Party."*

25. Do-nothings

It is our tradition that the young comrade, when he first approaches the party, with a little awe, often knowing little about it, is initially and provisionally educated with a few but lapidary slogans; one of these is "lead ass", which means that the ambitions of direct action, which unfortunately are not granted at this time, must be abandoned in the party. We are a party that in a considerable percentage of its activity, in a period that unfortunately has lasted for many decades, is dedicated to the study, the sculpting of theory and tactics. The recommendation was particularly necessary in the period between 1968 and the 70s of the past century, when youth rebellion was easily channeled into an activism without a future by organizations that referred to Marxism, organizations that have long since disappeared, or that have given place for opportunism and business. The desire to "come to blows", or even not to lose the "train of history", had also affected our party, and many wondered if the elephantine growth of groups such as Potere Operaio, Lotta Continua, and others, did not mean strategic errors of the party, errors that would have excluded us from the feast of a revolution that someone saw imminent. Suddenly we wanted new tactical indications to pass into the party, aimed at guaranteeing greater "appeal", an attractiveness towards young people that the "old" positions did not guarantee; although obviously this would have led to more people joinging (perhaps) on a different basis from those of our tradition, with consequences that were not difficult to foresee. Our call for greater adherence to the doctrine that we all shared was answered with isolation, calumny, and finally with expulsion.

26. The Reversal of Praxis

Returning to Lenin, at this point it is worthwhile to dwell on the relationship between the spontaneous movement of the proletariat and the party; between material drives that arise spontaneously within the society and revolutionary theoretical elaboration; between spontaneity and conscience. It is obvious that there would be no revolutionary theory if there had not been before large social movements to witness a contradiction between the mode of production and the demands of the workers, of any kind and condition. But the whole brochure tends to show the importance, the essentiality of a conscious guide for even extended movements to result in a revolutionary change of society. And at one point Lenin recalls that the conscious component of the class, the one he calls the ideologist, the party, can play an active role in the development of the revolutionary struggle, and not just a fatalistic expectation of the "*good moment*". *"They fail to understand that the "ideologist" is worthy of the name only when he precedes the spontaneous movement, points out the road, and is able ahead of all others to solve all the theoretical, political, tactical, and organizational questions which the "material elements" of the movement spontaneously encounter. … To say, however, that ideologists (i.e., politically conscious leaders* [read: the party]*) cannot divert the movement from the path determined by the interaction of environment and elements is to ignore the simple truth that the conscious element participates in this interaction and in the determination of the path."* (V, 316).

In our "Reversal of Praxis" concept, that the party enunciated at its inception, according to which the class party receives all stimuli and thrusts emanating from the mode of production and from the class, draws (has drawn) from it raw material for the elaboration of its doctrine, which eventually becomes guidelines for action to be reverberated on the class and on the individual worker: within certain limits, according to the situations and the force relationships, the party may take decisions and initiatives and influence the development of the struggle. The dialectical relationship lies in the fact that inasmuch as the revolutionary party is a conscious and voluntary factor of events, it is also a result of the same, and of the conflict they represent between ancient and new modes of production. A function destined to disappear if the material ties with the social environment and the class struggle were interrupted.

27. The Invariant Tactical Plan

An aspect the party reiterated in 1967 *"The continuity of action of the party, on the thread of the Left's tradition"*, Programma Comunista n. 3-5, 1967: "*… it is striking how for us not only are the problems of organization and functioning of the Marxist revolutionary party intertwined with the fundamental questions of doctrine, program and tactics, but also that the correct solution of the former is prejudicial to the correct setting and solution of the latter.*"

Obviously, that the party is a product of the environment in which it operates does not mean that the theory should be subjected to ups and downs according to the external situation: *"It is obvious that, while our party is a factor of events, it is at the same time a product of them; this also if we succeed in creating a really revolutionary world party. Now, in which sense do events reflect in this party? In the sense that the number of our members increases, and our influence on masses grows, when the crisis of capitalism engenders a situation favorable to us. If, on the contrary, at a given moment the situation becomes unfavorable, it may well be that our forces get reduced in number; but when that occurs we must not allow our ideology to suffer from it; not just our tradition, and our organization, but also our political line must remain intact."* (Third (Communist) International, 6th Enlarged Executive, Report by the Left of the C.P.of Italy; Fifth Session, 23/2/1926).

Continuing to point out how the party must work, and starting from the observations of economists, Lenin shows that there is no contradiction between the two statements made about Iskra:

"... Social-Democracy does not tie its hands, it does not restrict its activities to some one preconceived plan or method of political struggle; it recognizes all methods of struggle, provided they correspond to the forces at the disposal of the Party and facilitate the achievement of the best results possible under the given conditions...." (IV, 371).

and:

"...without a strong organization skilled in waging political struggle under all circumstances and at all times, there can be no question of that systematic plan of action, illumined by firm principles and steadfastly carried out, which alone is worthy of the name of tactics." (V, 18).

Then a plan, tactics, which is nothing more than describing what the party's attitude must be in given situations. The party must work, and this is the fundamental theoretical work of the party, to foresee the most varied scenarios in which it may find itself operating; not only the party as a whole, but also the individual militant, who may have to make important operational decisions in conditions of absent connection with the Center.

"...the fundamental error committed by the "new trend" in Russian Social-Democracy is its bowing to spontaneity and its failure to understand that the spontaneity of the masses demands a high degree of consciousness from us Social-Democrats. The greater the spontaneous upsurge of the masses and the more widespread the movement, the more rapid, incomparably so, the demand for greater consciousness in the theoretical, political and organizational work of Social-Democracy." (V, 396).

"Consciousness" means "knowledge", and it is exactly in this sense that Lenin means the term. Knowledge of the bourgeois world, in its politics, in its economy, in its culture, to be able to foresee the situations in which the party will find itself, to give indications of struggle to the working class. We, his humble students, have learned from him the need to work on the sculpting of theory and on the prediction of tactics to be adopted in the most varied, possible situations. This is the purpose of the work of the comrades, which periodically, at our General Meetings, is presented to the whole of the party; a job that serves not only to know, to know what to do in certain circumstances. Its importance is above all in sharing with all the comrades, who will know how to use it in a revolutionary sense. And in a continuous formation of the new militants, who get to acquire our doctrine in a natural way, rather than in ridiculous party schools. *"It would be nonsense to claim they are perfect texts, irrevocable and unchangeable"*, as we wrote in 1966 Theses of Naples *"because over the years the party has always said that it was material under continuous elaboration, destined to assume an ever better and more complete form"*. Texts that periodically get back, with new data and new details, on the principles that underlie our doctrine, without ever contradicting them. In this way the militants are always, through the participation to periodical, local and general meetings, in contact with our positions, and have the possibility to make them their own.

It is an ancient conviction of ours that a strong party is one whose militants, in a given situation, all behave in the same way even if they have no possibility of communicating with each other and with the center. Such is, however, the tradition of Marxism: *"The General Council feels proud of the prominent part the Paris branches of the International have taken in the glorious revolution of Paris. Not, as the imbeciles fancy, as if the Paris, or any other branch of the International received its mot d'ordre from a center. But the flower of the working class in all civilized countries belonging to the International, and being imbued with its ideas, they are sure everywhere in the working-class movement to take the lead.*" (Second draft of "The civil war in France", M-E, XXII, 545)

Theory is a single block, as we have already written, which does not change, but is sculpted, is always better defined. The tactic, on the other hand, is the provision of scenarios in which the party's response may have different implications, in the presence of events that are difficult to predict in detail; obviously the tactical choices depend on the knowledge of the data related to the various situations. Over time, and with the accumulation of knowledge on the basis of an ever-increasing record of struggle experiences, the space of tactical choices is reduced, and there are behaviors that from the tactical level, which offers choices, border on general theory, "dogmatic" and intangible. This is the case often cited of participation in political elections in countries with mature capitalism: the choice was placed until the 20s of the past century (even if for the Left sufficient experience already existed to reject it), today our doctrine excludes it , as a position on which there can be no doubt, a position that is part of our general theory.

Lenin does not believe that he has exhausted the spontaneity/consciousness argument, as the misunderstanding is very rooted in the socialist movement, not only in Russia and, we add, not only in 1902. So the third chapter, "Trade-Unionist Politics and Social-Democratic Politics ", is still dedicated to the controversy with economists, a subject that actually allows the establishment of precise boundaries to the activity of revolutionaries, clarifying their role in a situation of double revolution, when the bourgeois democratic revolution is still to be done.

28. Economic Struggle and Political Struggle

The defense of the economic conditions of the working class is necessary. But it cannot be considered, as economists do, the exclusive one. It is its school of war.

The danger, then as now, is that by focusing on sacrosanct activities, but in an exclusive way, one forgets the fundamental political tasks of the revolutionary socialist struggle: *"Social-Democracy leads the struggle of the working class, not only for better terms for the sale of labor-power, but for the abolition of the social system that compels the propertyless to sell themselves to the rich. Social-Democracy represents the working class, not in its relation to a given group of employers alone, but in its relation to all classes of modern society and to*

*the state as an organized political force. Hence, it
follows that not only must Social-Democrats not
confine themselves exclusively to the economic
struggle, but that they must not allow the
organization of economic exposures to become the
predominant part of their activities. We must take up
actively the political education of the working class
and the development of its political consciousness"*
(V, 400).

A consciousness that must include, in Russia,
the struggle to bring down the autocratic regime.
The struggle for social reforms, quite important for
the working class, is one of the duties of Social-
Democracy, which however "...*subordinates the
struggle for reforms, as the part to the whole, to the
revolutionary struggle for freedom and for
socialism.*" (V, 406).

The party therefore does not just elaborates a
program and a tactic to accomplish it; it also
evaluates, according to the historical moment, which
is the prevailing activity on which to spend its
resources and those of the class. Lenin explains to
factory workers that without a political change, of
the state power, their conditions would never
substantially improve, and that such improvement
would only be consolidated by the political victory
of their party, the one to manage power in their
behalf, up until a classless society.

Lenin never tires of insisting in supporting a
broader political agitation, to avoid a relapse in
economic *tailism*: "*Class political consciousness
can be brought to the workers only from without,*

that is, only from outside the economic struggle, from outside the sphere of relations between workers and employers." "To bring political knowledge to the workers *the Social Democrats must* go among all classes of the population; *they must dispatch units of their army* in all directions.... *the Social-Democrat's ideal should not be the trade union secretary, but the* tribune of the people." (V, 422-423).

What counts in this hammering that takes up most of the brochure is not so much the contingent polemic, a polemic that in any case might need to be resurrected even today, when within rank and file movements economist-type attitudes continue to resurface. What is important to note here is that Lenin, the supposed tactician, the allegedly astute navigator between congresses and currents, does not use half-words, does not rely on politicians' subtle words, but brands as bourgeois in no uncertain terms all that is not socialist and revolutionary: *"Trade-unionist politics of the working class is precisely* bourgeois politics *of the working class."* (V, 426).

He then goes on to describe the tasks of the Social Democrats in Russia, in that historical period, tasks that also include democratic objectives; but always calling them such, always distinguishing the activity of the party from that of other organizations, always, finally, clearly recalling what the party's ultimate goals are, even when it speaks to the other classes and social strata (peasants, students, clergy, artisans).

29. Workers Class Organs and the Communist Party

In the fourth chapter, "The Primitiveness of the Economists and the Organisation of the Revolutionaries", Lenin starts off by trying to explain the meaning of the term primitivism, retracing the recent history of social-democratic circles, and demonstrating how these have always been persecuted, and therefore destroyed, by the police, precisely because of a primitive, amateurish approach to the work; and does not hesitate to associate economists with this typology, who are primitive in that they underestimate the political and organizational tasks of the social democratic movement. Therefore it is necessary to refer to the theoretical and organizational cornerstones of a revolutionary party based on the working class.

First, we need to distinguish between workers' organization and the organization of revolutionaries: *"The workers' organizations for the economic struggle should be trade union organizations. Every Social-Democratic worker should as far as possible assist and actively work in these organizations. But, while this is true, it is certainly not in our interest to demand that only Social-Democrats should be eligible for membership in the "trade" unions, since that would only narrow the scope of our influence upon the masses. Let every worker who understands the need to unite for the struggle against the employers and the government join the trade unions.*

The very aim of the trade unions would be impossible of achievement, if they did not unite all who have attained at least this elementary degree of understanding, if they were not very broad organizations. The broader these organizations, the broader will be our influence over them — an influence due, not only to the "spontaneous" development of the economic struggle, but to the direct and conscious effort of the socialist trade union members to influence their comrades." (V, 454). So the trade union, because it is nothing else when it comes to corporative associations, must be composed only of workers; the Social-Democratic workers must work there, but it must not be expected that there be political unanimity within it; this sacrosanct principle, which as Lenin explains allows for very large and strong unions, then creates a particularly favorable environment for the revolutionary worker to carry out his propaganda. Those were years in which the mirage of revolutionary syndicalism was arising, in France (Sorel), in Italy, in South America, in the U.S.A. (I.W.W.), an experiment that after a couple of decades would show its failure, but that plagued the labor movement, preventing or making difficult the development of revolutionary parties of Marxist faith. Lenin predicts this degeneration of the movement, which could arise precisely from economists. As for the regime unions, like the famous one of Zubatov, he is not worried: *"Keep at it, gentlemen, do your best! Whenever you place a trap in the path of the workers (either by way of direct provocation, or by the "honest" demoralisation of the workers with the aid of "Struvism") we will see to it that you are exposed. But whenever you take a real step forward, though it be the most "timid zigzag", we will say: Please continue! And the only step that can be a real step forward is a real, if small, extension of the workers' field of action. Every such extension will be to our advantage and will help to hasten the advent of legal societies of the kind in which it will not be* agents provocateurs *who are detecting socialists, but socialists who are gaining adherents."* (V, 456).

Therefore, if these governmental, regime unions, want some favour among the workers, they will have to show that they deserve it, and what they will have to do will be their legalization; but in doing so they will create favorable conditions for the revolutionary and union activity of the Social Democrats. Moreover, workers who constitute secret trade unions will also have to be helped, because the true struggle, even in trade unions, requires clandestinity; this too is a fundamental task of the revolutionaries.

The important thing is not to talk to the workers in a generic, unrealistic, or improvised way; it would be demagoguery, says Lenin, and in the long run this would alienate us from the favours of the proletarians. The speaker must know what he says.

Both the trade union and the political struggle require organization, but the two spheres are very different, and so are the methods of organization, and not just in a police regime like that of the beginning of XX century in Russia. The party must rely on professional revolutionaries, not amateur politicians, and in this way it will be better defended by police persecutions, and its propaganda and agitation will be truly effective. The necessity of clandestinity leads to the centralization of clandestine work, but this "*by no means implies centralization of all the functions of the* movement" (V, 465). The party in this sense does not give itself fixed schematic rules, but adapts its organization to the conditions in which it operates.

30. Workers and Intellectuals in the Party

It is therefore a question of forming revolutionaries, but we must also be able to draw from the ranks of the class, and not only from the intellectuals: "*… our very first and most pressing duty is to help to train working-class revolutionaries who will be on the same level in regard to Party activity as the revolutionaries from amongst the intellectuals (we emphasise the words "in regard to Party activity", for, although necessary, it is neither so easy nor so pressingly necessary to bring the workers up to the level of intellectuals in other respects). Attention, therefore, must be devoted principally to raising the workers to the level of revolutionaries; it is not at all our task to descend to the level of the "working masses" as the Economists wish to do*" (V, 470).

Although Lenin always recognizes that from an organizational point of view the role of the working class has been decisive. This, thanks to objective economic causes, is distinguished from all classes of capitalist society by its greater aptitude for organization. *What is to be done?* stresses that without the contact with the working class the organization of the revolutionaries would have been a toy, an adventure, an empty symbol, and that only when there is a "*truly revolutionary class that spontaneously rises to the struggle*" does the organization that the party advocates for the moment of proletarian assault make sense.

But to do this we need real persons who are dedicated to creating this organization.

Revolutionaries by profession, true militants, disciplined and no big mouths, avant-garde rooted in the class and able to direct it: these are the members of the party for Lenin. Beyond the contingent situations, Lenin fights against opportunism in organizational matters: party members must not be talkative, i.e., revolutionary in words, but militants who do not just participate in the movement from time to time, when they have desire, "*to go to meetings on free evenings*".

31. Conspirativism and Terrorism

Even terrorism, which was still gaining support, was to be associated to the spontaneist swamp: *"The Economists and the present-day terrorists have one common root, namely,* subservience to spontaneity." *"The road to hell is paved with good intentions, and, in this case, good intentions cannot save one from being spontaneously drawn "along the line of least resistance""* [here again the concept we always shared] *"… calls for terror and calls to lend the economic struggle itself a political character are merely two different forms of evading the most pressing duty now resting upon Russian revolutionaries, namely, the organization of comprehensive political agitation"* (V, 418, 420).

Against the apostles of conspiracy Lenin is explicit: *"We have always protested, and will, of course, continue to protest against confining the political struggle to conspiracy. But this does not, of course, mean that we deny the need for a strong revolutionary organization."* (V, 475). *"Only a centralized, militant organization that consistently carries out a Social-Democratic policy, that satisfies, so to speak, all revolutionary instincts and strivings, can safeguard the movement against*

*making thoughtless attacks and prepare attacks that
hold out the promise of success."* (V, 477).

32. The Organic Selection of Leaders

To the accusations of lack of internal democracy
the reply is simple: you ask for a large democracy in
a situation of clandestinity, instead of a strict secret
and a rigorous selection!

However, it is also clear that Lenin does not
refer to an absolute *democratic principle* but to the
banal *mechanism* by which comrades in the party are
elected to the various functions. *Electing* does not
only mean *voting,* but choosing, selecting. And in
Lenin's words, if well understood, is not the defense
of the mechanism but of the substance of the party's
organic functioning.

Lenin here addresses the Russians, for whom the
European parties must also be an example of
organization. He tells them that in a country that is
not feudal but bourgeois and democratic, where
freedom of speech exists, the party can function
according to its modules, where those who run for
office are known to all. *"…consequently, all party
members, knowing all the facts, can elect or refuse
to elect this person to a particular party office. The
general control (in the literal sense of the term)
exercised over every act of a party man in the
political field brings into existence an automatically*

operating mechanism which produces what in biology is called the "survival of the fittest". "Natural selection" by full publicity, election, and general control provides the assurance that, in the last analysis, every political figure will be "in his proper place", do the work for which he is best fitted by his powers and abilities, feel the effects of his mistakes on himself, and prove before all the world his ability to recognize mistakes and to avoid them...".

Lenin goes on to refer to a non-democratic regime, such as the Russian one at the time. But history would soon confirm that very little "democracy" will be enjoyed by the revolutionary communists in Germany, in Italy... His words, correctly understood, surpass and deny even the adoption of the democratic mechanism within the party.

But in a regime such as the Russian, a "broad democracy" *"...is nothing more than a* useless *and* harmful toy. *It is a useless toy because, in point of fact, no revolutionary organization has ever practiced, or could practice, broad democracy, however much it may have desired to do so. It is a harmful toy because any attempt to practise "the broad democratic principle" will simply facilitate the work of the police in carrying out large-scale raids, will perpetuate the prevailing primitiveness, and will divert the thoughts of the practical workers from the serious and pressing task of training themselves to become professional revolutionaries to that of drawing up detailed "paper" rules for election systems. Only abroad, where very often people with no opportunity for conducting really active work gather, could this "playing at democracy" develop here and there, especially in small groups ".*

33. The Need for Complete Confidence between Revolutionaries

"The only serious organizational principle for the active workers of our movement should he the strictest secrecy, the strictest selection of members, and the training of professional revolutionaries. Given these qualities, something even more than "democratism" would be guaranteed to us, namely, complete, comradely, mutual confidence among revolutionaries. This is absolutely essential for us, because there can be no question of replacing it by general democratic control in Russia.

It would be a great mistake to believe that the impossibility of establishing real "democratic" [inverted commas are Lenin's] *control renders the members of the revolutionary organization beyond control altogether. They have not the time to think about toy forms of democratism (democratism within a close and compact body of comrades in which complete, mutual confidence prevails), but they have a lively sense of their responsibility, knowing as they do from experience that an organization of real revolutionaries will stop at nothing to rid itself of an unworthy member. Moreover, there is a fairly well-developed public opinion in Russian (and international) revolutionary circles which has a long history behind it, and which sternly and ruthlessly punishes every departure from the duties of comradeship (and "democratism", real and not toy democratism, certainly forms a component part of the conception of comradeship). Take all this into consideration and you will realise that this talk and these resolutions about "anti-democratic tendencies" have the musty odour of the playing at generals which is indulged in abroad."* (V, 479-481)

It is evident here that with "real democratism" Lenin means nothing but the organic unity of the party.

Not very different is what the party writes in 1922, in the Rome Theses, I, 4: *"The announcement of these programmatic declarations, and the appointment of the humans to whom are entrusted the various positions in the party organization, is formally carried out by means of a consultation, democratic in form, of the party's representative assemblies, but in reality they must be understood as a product of the real process which accumulates elements of experience and realizes the preparation and selection of leaders, thus shaping both the programmatic content and the hierarchical constitution of the party."*

The organicity that must orient the party when it comes to choose the comrades to whom to entrust party responsibilities is also visible in the comment

Lenin makes about the choice of the components of the Iskra editorial board, i.e., of the comrades who were to constitute the party " center": *"The old board of six was so ineffectual that never once in all its three years did it meet in full force. That may seem incredible, but it is a fact. Not one of the forty-five issues of* Iskra *was made up (in the editorial and technical sense) by anyone but Martov or Lenin. And never once was any major theoretical issue raised by anyone but Plekhanov. Axelrod did no work at all (he contributed literally nothing to Zarya and only three or four articles to all the forty-five issues of* Iskra). *Zasulich and Starover only contributed and advised, they never did any actual editorial work. Who ought to be elected to the* political leadership, *to the* c e n t r e, *was as clear as daylight to every delegate at the Congress, after the month it had been in session."* (VII, 31).

We had to put together these long quotations, which are of good help to clarify Lenin's thought on the matter, and which therefore do not require interpretation. However, we like to highlight that the thought of the great Vladimir is one thing with the way of existence of the present party of the Left. First of all, there is an ill-concealed disdain for democracy, a "toy" for opportunists to put hurdles in the way of party's activity. Secondly, the functioning of the party is presented as that of an organism, in which the comrade is in the function that is organically more suited to him; the juxtaposition, if not the identification of the "organically" adverb with what we called "organic centralism" at the dawn of the Left, and that our party still practices is obvious. Hence, comrades who have their organic place in the party, fraternal consideration and trust among comrades, equally organic processes for identifying shortcomings or out and out betrayals. It is the problem of "guarantees", which we have often faced in our texts. Democratism invoked as a panacea is a form of primitivism, and therefore by now (in 1902!) of opportunism. Also in "*Letter to a Comrade on Our Organizational Tasks*" of 1902 Lenin is careful not to invoke democratic statutes or organizational norms, but identifies the solution to problems of individuals (including efficiency and operational capacity) in fraternal relations between comrades, and as a last resort in the appeal to the central organ, which for him obviously represents the doctrine of the party, the corpus of the theory of revolution, the only real level able to settle all the questions that may arise.

Immediately after the Second Congress, instead of railing against Martov for leaving the editorial office, and prefiguring a split (which there will be), Lenin concludes his *"Account of the Second Congress of the R.S.D.L.P."* with a reminder for all comrades to the true values of party work, far more than bureaucratic and democratic formalisms: *"The Russian Social-Democratic movement is in the throes of the last difficult transition from the circles to a Party, from philistinism to a realisation of revolutionary duty, from acting by means of scandal-mongering and circle pressure to discipline. Anyone who values Party work and action in the interests of the Social-Democratic labor movement will refuse to tolerate such wretched sophistries as a "legitimate" and "loyal" boycott of the central bodies; he will not allow the cause to suffer and the work to be brought to a standstill because a dozen or so individuals are displeased that they and their friends were not elected to the central bodies; he will not allow Party officials to be subjected to private and secret pressure through threats of non-collaboration, through boycotts, through cutting off of funds, through scandal-mongering and lying tales."* (VII, 34).

34. We do not Love Anyone, but we Love Everyone

This does not mean, however, that relations between comrades should be guided by "sentimentalism", an aspect in which he dwells in recounting the experience of his first encounter with Plechanov (IV, 342), from which he emerged disappointed by the person, but strengthened in his determination to go ahead anyway. In "*Politique d'abord*" of 1952 the party draws the same conclusions: *"A long and tragic experience should therefore have taught that in party activity we must utilize each militant according to his particular attitudes and possibilities, but that "we must not love anyone", and be ready to throw away anyone, even if he had done eleven months in prison each year of his life. We must be able to take the decision on the options for action in front of momentous events outside the personal "authority" of masters, leaders and executives, and based on the pre-established norms of principle and action of our movement: an extremely difficult endeavour, as we all know, but without which one cannot see how a powerful movement may reappear."*

35. Internal Hierarchy and Decision Making

Proof of Lenin's consideration for internal democracy can be found in what Trotzkij reports in "*My life*"; it was at the onset of the II Congress:

"*… one of the important points in the scheme of organization was the relationship to be established between the central organ (the* Iskra*) and the Central Committee which was to function in Russia. I arrived abroad with the belief that the editorial board should be made subordinate to the Central Committee. This was the prevailing attitude of the majority of the Iskra followers. "It can't be done" objected Lenin. "The correlation of forces is different. How can they guide us from Russia? No, it can't be done. We are the stable center, we are stronger in ideas, and we must exercise the guidance from here". "Then this will mean a complete dictatorship of the editorial board? " I asked. "Well, what's wrong with that?" retorted Lenin. "In the present situation it must be so".*"

It is not respect for democratic rules that keeps the party on the right track, but complete and stubborn adherence to Marxist doctrine! And that Lenin, alone, personified at that time. The doctrine was in the central organ, that is, in the historical party; how can the best revolutionary work result from a democratic consultation, or worse, from a mediation between different currents, which unfortunately existed in Lenin's party?

Lenin on this is very clear again in 1920, when the Workers' Opposition demanded that decisions be taken on the basis of proportional representation in the Central Committee and in the various city committees. And that democracy should be utilized to solve operational problems: *"…proportional representation is essential in calling a Party conference as a directing body, or a Party congress. When, however, it is a question of setting up an executive body charged with the conduct of practical work, proportional representation has never been applied, and can hardly be considered justified.. …. the decisive consideration must be that you, members of this Conference, should have a personal knowledge of each candidate, and give preference to that group which may be expected to work harmoniously, and not the principle of proportionality in the election of an executive body, a principle that has never been applied, and to apply which would hardly be right at present."* (XXXI, 428).

We have already seen that for Lenin internal democracy was inevitable, but also that when it comes to operational decisions, and even when it comes to stating the founding positions of the party, democracy is a useless, and even harmful, tinsel which the great Vladimir is willing to do without.

We, thanks to the experience of further decades of counter-revolution and betrayal by the so-called Leninists, got rid completely of democracy, in all its forms. In the party it is customary to state the paradox that democracy could have meaning if at the same time could vote the living, the dead and the children of future generations!

36. The Guarantees

Since the party body is formed on the basis of voluntary adhesion, the "guarantee" that the strictest discipline is obtained must therefore be sought in the clear definition of the unique, and binding for all, tactical rules, in the continuity of the methods of struggle and in the clarity of the organizational rules. In *Marxism and authority* (1956) we wrote: *"We will just remind the guarantees that we have so often proposed and illustrated, also in the* Dialogue with the Dead. *Doctrine: the Center has no faculty to change it from that established, from the beginning, in the classic texts of the movement. Organization: unique internationally, it does not vary for aggregations or mergers, but only for individual admissions; the organized members cannot join other movements. Tactics: the possibilities of maneuver and action must be foreseen by decisions of international congresses with a closed system. At*

*the base you cannot start actions not arranged by
the center: the center cannot invent new tactics and
moves, under the pretext of new facts. The link
between the party base and the center becomes a
dialectical form. If the party exercises the
dictatorship of the class in the state, and against the
classes against which the state acts, there is no
dictatorship of the center of the party on the basis.
The dictatorship is not denied with a formal internal
mechanical democracy, but with respect for those
dialectical ties."*

37. An All-Russia Political Newspaper

Also counterposing local work with national
work indicates, in those who defend the former, a
form of primitivism. Local work also languishes
because there is no national activity plan, an aspect
that Lenin will clarify better in the fifth and last
chapter, although in reality he spends many pages
demonstrating with historical data what he argues.
Rather than supporting the local press, there is a
need for a nationwide organ, "specialized" on union
work and agitation.

*The "Plan" For an All-Russia Political
Newspaper*: here too an answer is given to criticisms
against the creation of a press organ that collects the
contributions of all the committees and circles (they
were not yet sections of a single party) point by
point. It is clear that for Lenin a newspaper for the

whole of Russia is very close to the idea that he has of the party of the revolution; initially the object is the newspaper, but from his words it soon appears that in the structure of the press organ he sees the embryo of the party, which moves in the police regime of the time; because in the end the fundamental and urgent need is precisely that of a Marxist, revolutionary party, with a solid theoretical basis, shared by the whole organization, precisely through an organ that all militants read and from which they take the material for their propaganda.

So nothing to do with debates and runways of opinions, but a newspaper worthy of the orthodox revolutionary Marxist party; after a reminder of the need to define oneselves before joining, in "*Declaration of the Editorial Board of Iskra*" Lenin clarifies without possibility of equivocation: "*…we do not intend to make our publication a mere storehouse of various views. On the contrary, we shall conduct it in the spirit of a strictly defined tendency. This tendency can be expressed by the word Marxism, and there is hardly need to add that we stand for the* **consistent** *development of the ideas of Marx and Engels* [our sculpting!] *and emphatically reject the equivocating, vague, and opportunist "corrections" for which Eduard Bernstein, P. Struve, and many others have set the fashion.*" (IV, 354-355).

Once made this clear, what should the newspaper be for? "*We should not only be clear on the nature of the organization that is needed and its precise purpose, but we must elaborate a definite plan for an organization, so that its formation may be undertaken from all aspects." "A newspaper is what we most of all need; without it we cannot conduct that systematic, all-round propaganda and agitation, consistent in principle, which is the chief and permanent task of Social-Democracy in general and, in particular, the pressing task of the moment, when interest in politics and in questions of socialism has been aroused among the broadest strata of the population." "It may be said without exaggeration that the frequency and regularity with which a newspaper is printed (and distributed) can serve as a precise criterion of how well this cardinal and most essential sector of our militant activities is built up."*

"The role of a newspaper, however, is not limited solely to the dissemination of ideas, to political education, and to the enlistment of political allies. A newspaper is not only a collective propagandist and a collective agitator, it is also a collective organizer". "With the aid of the newspaper, and through it, a permanent organization will naturally lake shape that will engage, not only in local activities, but in regular general work, and will train its members to follow political events carefully, appraise their significance and their effect on the various strata of the population, and develop effective means for the revolutionary party to influence these events. The mere technical task of regularly supplying the newspaper with copy and of promoting regular distribution will necessitate a network of local

agents of the united party, who will maintain constant contact with one another, know the general state of affairs, get accustomed to performing regularly their detailed functions in the All-Russian work, and test their strength in the organization of various revolutionary actions. This network of agents will form the skeleton of precisely the kind of organization we need" "With the aid of the newspaper, and through it, a permanent organization will naturally take shape that will engage, not only in local activities, but in regular general work, and will train its members to follow political events carefully, appraise their significance and their effect on the various strata of the population, and develop effective means for the revolutionary party to influence these events. The mere technical task of regularly supplying the newspaper with copy and of promoting regular distribution will necessitate a network of local agents of the united party, who will maintain constant contact with one another, know the general state of affairs, get accustomed to performing regularly their detailed functions in the All-Russian work, and test their strength in the organization of various revolutionary actions. This network of agents will form the skeleton of precisely the kind of organization we need." (V, 20-23).

"... the whole point is that there is no other way of training strong political organizations except through the medium of an all-Russia newspaper.".. "All without exception now talk of the importance of unity, of the necessity for

"gathering and Organizing"; but in the majority of cases what is lacking is a definite idea of where to begin and how to bring about this unity."..."I continue to insist that we can* start establishing *real contacts only with the aid of a common newspaper, as the only regular, all-Russia enterprise, one which will summarise the results of the most diverse forms of activity and thereby* stimulate *people to march forward untiringly along* all *the innumerable paths leading to revolution, in the same way as all roads lead to Rome. If we do not want unity in name only, we must arrange for all local study circles* immediately to assign, *say, a fourth of their forces* to active *work for the* common *cause." ... "In a great many cases these forces are now being bled white on restricted local work, but under the circumstances we are discussing it would be possible to transfer a capable agitator or organiser from one end of the country to the other, and the occasion for doing this would constantly arise. Beginning with short journeys on Party business at the Party's expense, the comrades would become accustomed to being maintained by the Party, to becoming professional revolutionaries, and to* training themselves as real political leaders."..." *Around what is in itself still a very innocuous and very small, but regular and* common, *effort, in the full sense of the word, a regular army of tried fighters would systematically gather and receive their training.* [to rouse the whole people]... *That is what we should dream of!"* (V, 499-509).

38. Good Tactics and a Good Party

Which are the characteristic features of this organization? The ability to foretell in its main lines the course of events: *"Those who make nation-wide political agitation the cornerstone of their program,* their tactics, and their organizational work, *as* Iskra *does, stand the least risk of missing the revolution. The people who are now engaged throughout Russia in weaving the network of connections that spread from the all-Russia newspaper not only did not miss the spring events, but, on the contrary, gave us an opportunity to foretell them. … And if they live they will not miss the revolution, which, first and foremost, will demand of us experience in agitation, ability to support (in a Social-Democratic manner) every protest, as well as direct the spontaneous movement, while safeguarding it from the mistakes of friends and the traps of enemies."*

Flexibility: *"Only such organization will ensure the* flexibility *required of a militant Social-Democratic organization, viz., the ability to adapt itself immediately to the most diverse and rapidly changing conditions of struggle"*

Contempt for haste, impatience, typical of the bourgeois society (see also above): *"Unless we are able to devise political tactics and* an organizational plan for work over a very long period, *while ensuring,* in the very process of this work, *our Party's readiness to be at its post and fulfil its duty in every contingency whenever the march of events is accelerated — unless we succeed in doing this, we shall prove to be but miserable political adventurers. Only Nadezhdin, who began but yesterday to describe himself as a Social-Democrat, can forget that the aim of Social-Democracy is to transform radically the conditions of life of the whole of mankind and that for this reason it is not permissible for a Social-Democrat to be "perturbed" by the question of the duration of the work."*

Carrying out all party duties: "*...the revolution must be regarded...as a series of more or less powerful outbreaks rapidly alternating with periods of more or less complete calm. For that reason, the principal content of the activity of our Party organization, the focus of this activity, should be work that is both possible and essential in the period of a most powerful outbreak as well as in the period of complete calm." "Our wiseacre fails to see that it is precisely during the revolution that we shall stand in need of the results of our theoretical battles with the Critics in order to be able resolutely to combat their practical positions!"*

Organic structuring of work: "*But a network of agents that would form in the course of establishing and distributing the common newspaper would not have to "sit about and wait" for the call for an uprising, but could carry on the regular activity that would guarantee the highest probability of success in the event of an uprising. Such activity would strengthen our contacts with the broadest strata of the working masses and with all social strata that are discontented with the autocracy."*

Therefore: *"In a word, the "plan for an all-Russia political newspaper", far from representing the fruits of the labor of armchair workers, infected with dogmatism and bookishness … is the most practical plan for immediate and all-round preparation of the uprising, with, at the same time, no loss of sight for a moment of the pressing day-to-day work."* (V, 513-516).

The mere technical task of guarding, disseminating and delivering, etc. the newspaper needs frameworks at central level that guarantee the correct organization of this body and trustees in local groups.

39. Communist Centralism vs. Class Dispersion Within Bourgeois Society

Ultimately it is a question of creating an organization as a premise and not as a result of the revolutionary process; or, if you will, as a result of an already advanced revolutionary process that began with the birth and opposition of the bourgeoisie and the proletariat many centuries ago.

This was not understood by the Mensheviks in 1903, when they provoked their separation from the majority group which made reference to Lenin. A letter of Axelrod to Kautsky, of June 6, 1904, is quite explicit on the matter. In short, Axelrod believes that the situation in Russia is not mature for the birth of an organized party, structured in view of seizing the power. He ridicules Lenin's organizational perspective as *"…trivial and pitiable caricature of the autocratic-bureaucratic system of our Ministry of the Interiors"*. *"Organizational fetishism"*, which would cause the *"misunderstanding"* that led to the split. But in a point he sees clearly, although wrongly interpreting: *"The divergencies among us on organizational problems arose for the first time in a clear and concrete way only with reference to the methods and procedures utilized by Lenin and his supporters to practically enforce "centralism", which we all admit…"*. Those very methods and procedures are the only real guarantee of both party correct functioning, and of the maintenance of its orthodoxy.

The pamphlet ends with a brief summary of the three stages of social democracy in Russia, and with the hope that there will be a fourth, with the exit from the crisis and with the strengthening of militant Marxism. Lenin wishes it, we know that it will be thanks above all to his powerful and tireless work. Which is mainly aimed at creating an organization worthy of the name. Thus he concludes *"One Step Forward, Two Steps Back"*: *"In its struggle for power the proletariat has no other weapon but organization. Disunited by the rule of anarchic competition in the bourgeois world, ground down by forced labor for capital, constantly thrust back to the "lower depths" of utter destitution, savagery, and degeneration, the proletariat can, and inevitably will, become an invincible force only through its ideological unification on the principles of Marxism being reinforced by the material unity of organization, which welds millions of toilers into an army of the working class. Neither the senile rule of the Russian autocracy nor the senescent rule of international capital will be able to withstand this army. It will more and more firmly close its ranks, in spite of all zigzags and backward steps, in spite of the opportunist phrase-mongering of the Girondists of present-day Social-Democracy, in spite of the self-satisfied exaltation of the retrograde circle spirit, and in spite of the tinsel and fuss of intellectualist anarchism."* (VII, 412-413).

40. Organic Centralism

Although he operates in an age and in an environment in which the democratic method had not yet clearly demonstrated to the party how unsuitable it was for its functioning, what we have seen so far demonstrates, to those who want to understand, that Lenin, based on his critical observation of the working mechanisms of the socialist parties, takes sides with a way of being of the party that we can now define as "organic" and "centralistic". If centralism and organizational discipline are the condition for the existence of the communist party as such, such a condition cannot be obtained with the mechanisms of the bourgeois parties. Even in its functioning the working class party is forced to be revolutionary.

The way of being of the party will be formulated by the comrades of the Left since the birth of the Communist Party of Italy, Section of the III International.

In the following years the experience of the Stalinist counter-revolution was the clear proof that that of organic centralism was the only method to give the party a chance to survive, even organizationally, in periods of revolutionary reflux. Enunciated again in 1926, at the III Congress of P.C.d'I. (Lyon), organic centralism is reaffirmed at all times when the party finds itself in difficult turns: in the post-war period, in 1952, in 1965, in 1973. It is only thanks to a close, almost fanatical adherence to our way of work, that the party is still active and in good health 68 years after its reconstitution in 1952, where in good health means being tied to the doctrinal cornerstones that were of Marx, Engels, Lenin and the Left.

What, then, is in short organic centralism? We will certainly not deny ourselves by giving here a series of rules, a code, a regulation or, worse, a statute. Rather, we will recall some cornerstones of our way of working, already partly outlined in the text we've been commenting so far, citing the party at various times of its existence. Without forgetting that our history teaches us that the acquisition of our method cannot derive from bookish descriptions, however detailed they may be; the comrade masters the working method of the party by working inside it, in its "ferociously anti-bourgeois" ambient, which puts together all types of comrades and of generations. With the additional difficulty that in our case he must get rid of a mass of cultural-ideological dead weight, soaked with the myth of the individual, of the homeland and of divinity, with which the boundless means of bourgeois society have poisoned the depth of his soul.

However, it must be preliminarily clarified that the internal forms of behavior of the Communist Party do not respond to commandments, aesthetic canons or abstract moral norms, but are the teachings of a painful past that has seen in their denial the poison administered to the party to accompany its degeneration until the passage to the enemy. Moreover, a coherent internal organic life, among comrades who "hold hands closely", is a coefficient of strength, a material fact, that comes before conscience and affection, a discipline that in social warfare gives the Party that effective unity of intent and movement that is denied to every bourgeois organism and institution.

41. Democratic Centralism

Firstly, the formal rules that guarantee the functioning of democratic centralism should be remembered, what all "left wingers" oppose to organic centralism. The differences existing within the party can only be solved by the balance of power: the differences present within the leadership cannot be resolved but with political struggle;

election of the governing bodies with a democratic
mechanism, that is, with the counting of votes; right
to the formation of tendencies before the election of
the steering organs and before the congress; regular
convening of congresses; right to periodic
verification of majority decisions in the light of
experiences made, i.e., the right of minorities to
attempt periodically to rectify majority decisions;
right to organize into currents and fractions, etc.

In short, democratic centralism, raised as a
principle against Lenin, sanctions the non-marxist
principle of the continuous reconstruction of theory
and tactics, in periodic congresses, on the basis of
purported changes in the social, economic and
political conditions of society, of course all
conditions that would vary from country to country,
if not actually modulated for particular areas within
individual countries. The choices are not determined
on the basis of an intangible program, nor on the
basis of historical and scientific evidence, but on the
basis of the majority gathered around a given
solution.

Lenin, while he cannot avoid some of these
rules, and even puts them forward as a first
instrument against dispersion and indiscipline of
circles, is continually accused of hindering, for his
excessive centralism, the development of internal
party democracy.

In 1972, we compared the two centralisms in
this way (*Introduction to the theses after 1945*, by *In
defense of the continuity of the communist program*,
p. 130): "In truth, the question of organic centralism

as opposed to democratic centralism is far from being ... terminological. In its contradictory nature, the second formula reflects, in the noun, the aspiration to the single world party as we have always hoped for, but reflects in the adjective the reality of parties still heterogeneous in historical formation and doctrinal basis."

"In our view, on the other hand, the party presents itself with characters of organic centrality because it is not a "part", albeit the most advanced, of the proletarian class, but its organ, synthesizer of all its elementary thrusts as of all its militants, from whichever direction they come from, and this is due to the possession of a theory, a set of principles, a program, which bypass the time limits of today to express the historical trend, the final goal and the way of working of the proletarian and communist generations of the past, present and future, and who go beyond the boundaries of nationality and state to embody the interests of revolutionary workers of the whole world; such is, we add, also by virtue of a forecast, at least in broad terms, of the unfolding of historical situations, and therefore of the ability to establish a body of directives and tactical rules that are mandatory for everyone (obviously, not without considering the times and areas of "double revolution" or, instead, of "pure proletarian revolution", also foreseen and implying a very precise, even if different, tactical behavior). If the party is in possession of such theoretical and practical homogeneity (possession that is not guaranteed forever, but a reality to be defended tooth

and nail and, if necessary, to reconquer every time),
its organization, which is at the same time its
discipline, is born and develops *organically* on the
unitary line of the program and of practical action,
and expresses in its different forms of realization, in
the hierarchy of its organs, the perfect adherence of
the party to the complex of its functions, none
excluded."

42. The Left's Centralism

We have a first enunciation in 1922 (*The
Democratic Principle*): "*Democracy cannot be a
principle for us: centralism indisputably is, since the
essential characteristics of party organization must
be unity of structure and action. In order to express
the continuity of party structure in space, the term
centralism is sufficient, but in order to introduce the
essential idea of continuity in time – the historical
continuity of the struggle which, surmounting
successive obstacles, always advances towards the
same goal – we will propose saying, linking these
two essential ideas of unity together, that the
communist party bases its organization on "organic
centralism""*.

In 1926, in a situation of retreat and loss of the
revolutionary compass by the international party, of
which we were perfectly aware, the Left reiterated
the importance of the correct management of the
party:

"*II.5 -…. The communist parties must achieve
an organic centralism, which, whilst including as*

much consultation with the base as possible, ensures the spontaneous elimination of any grouping which starts to differentiate itself. This cannot be achieved by means of the formal and mechanical prescriptions of a hierarchy, but, as Lenin says [in *Left-wing communism*, ed.], *by means of correct revolutionary politics.*" (Draft Theses presented by the Left at the IIIrd Congress of P.C.d'I., Lyon 1926).

In short, the party must be a centralized structure, with the existence of different organs and of a central body capable of coordinating, directing and ordering the whole network; absolute discipline of all members of the organization in executing orders placed by the center; no autonomy to local sections or groups; no communication network diverging from the unitary one that connects the center to the periphery and the periphery to the center. And the neverending activity of study, of sculpturing of the doctrine, which is peculiar to the party, does not only have a theoretical value, it is also, and above all, an organizational necessity, in order to be at any time able to express the 'correct revolutionary politics'.

43. How the Party is Structured According to Lenin

Not very different is what Lenin advocates in"*Letter to a Comrade on Our Organizational Tasks*" (VI, 234, 249-250): "*… the newspaper can and should be the ideological leader of the Party,*

*evolving theoretical truths, tactical principles,
general organizational ideas, and the general tasks
of the whole Party at any given moment." (...)*

*"And it is not merely because revolutionary
work does not always lend itself to definite
organizational form that Rules are useless. No,
definite organizational form is necessary, and we
must endeavour to give such* form *to all our work as
far as possible. That is permissible to a much
greater extent than is generally thought, and
achievable not through Rules but solely and
exclusively (we must keep on reiterating this)
through transmitting exact information to the Party
center; it is only then that we shall have real
organizational form connected with real
responsibility and (inner-Party) publicity. "*

We recall that, as we saw in "*What is to be
done?*", when Lenin says newspaper, magazine,
Iskra (when he is in it), he means the center of the
party, which in 1902 is above all the ideological,
doctrinal center of the party. Every reference to the
central organ means a reference to orthodox
Marxism, as presented to the various circles by the
theoretical work of Lenin himself and of the others
of *Iskra*. So he already speaks of dictatorship of the
program, and not of men, even though we know that
at that moment the true revolutionary doctrine
resided in the work of an individual; incidentally, a
negative aspect, as an index of party's vulnerability,
and it will be manifest after the premature death of
the great Vladimir, when a clear military defeat
would have been historically more desirable, rather

than a triumph of the counter-revolution passed through a degeneration of the Russian party, of the International and of all the national sections.

44. Avoid Splits with Joint and Unanimous Work

We gather another testimony of Lenin, which as we will see coincides with the Left's way of working:

"To the question—"what should not be done?" (what should not be done in general, and what, in particular, should not be done so as to avoid a split), my reply is, first of all: do not conceal from the Party the appearance and growth of potential causes of a split, do not conceal any of the circumstances and events that constitute such causes; and, what is more, do not conceal them not only from the Party, but, as far as possible, from the outside public either. … Broad publicity—that is the surest, the only reliable means of avoiding such splits as can be avoided, and of reducing to a minimum the harm of splits that are no longer avoidable.." "Letter to "*Iskra*"" (VII, 115-116).

Again in 1920, at a party conference, while still fighting against the armies of whites, faced with the difficulties posed by the Workers Opposition, Lenin, while conceding those comrades some good point, insisted above all that the whole party be involved in solving the problem; but at the same time he recalls that there is a program, which must be respected at all costs, if we don't want to succumb to the enemy. *"The opposition ... no doubt contains a sound element, but when it turns into an opposition for the sake of opposition, we should certainly put an end to it. We have wasted a great deal of time on altercations, quarrels and recrimination and we must put an end to all that, and try to come to some agreement to work more effectively. We must make certain concessions ... but we must succeed in making our work harmonious, for otherwise we cannot exist when we are surrounded by enemies at home and abroad."* (XXXI, 424).

Therefore strict adherence to the programmatic cornerstones, with well-known criteria, always repeated to all, not only in section meetings, but also in the press; to solve problems collectively, after which total executive discipline, without complaints about lack of democracy.

"It is around this inseparable and very hard core, doctrine-program-tactic, a collective and impersonal heritage of the movement, that our organization is crystallized, and what holds it together is not the knut of the "organizing center" but the unique and uniform thread linking "leaders" and "base", "center" and "periphery", committing them to the observance and defense of a system of ends and means, none of which is separable from the other. *In this real life of the communist party - not of* any *party but only of it as it is communist in* deeds *and not in* name - *the puzzle that haunts the bourgeois democrat; who decides: the "top" or the*

*"bottom", the most or the few? Who "commands"
and who "obeys"? (...)*

*"The generous concern of the comrades that the
party should operate in an organizational, safe,
linear and homogeneous manner, should therefore
address - as Lenin himself admonished in the "Letter
to a Comrade on Our Organizational Tasks" - not a
search for statutes, codes and constitutions, or
worse, for personalities of "special" temperament,
but rather the best way to contribute, each and every
one, to the harmonious performance of the functions
without which the party would cease to exist as a
unifying force and as guide and representation of
the class, which is the only way to help it to solve,
day by day, "by itself", - as in "What is to be
done?", where the newspaper is referred to as a
"collective organizer" - its problems of life and
action. Here is the key to "organic centralism," here
is the sure weapon in the historic battle of the
classes, not in the empty abstraction of the alleged
"norms" of the functioning of the most perfect
mechanisms or, worse, in the squalor of trials of
humans who by organic selection found themselves
handling them."* (The Continuity of Party Action on
the Thread of the Left's Tradition, Programma
Comunista, 3-5/1967).

45. How to Guarantee Discipline?

The party functions thanks to the work of humans; what are the guarantees that these humans will not betray, or make mistakes? The objection of the petty bourgeois is evident: who will prevent individuals from doing whatever they like, from disobeying, because in every individual, even militant in the party, there is the germ of individualism, self-exaltation, anarchism, etc.? Who will prevent individuals from raising problems just for the sake of doing it, or from making criticisms? The Left has already answered over 50 years ago to objections of this kind and the answer sounds like this: in an organism, like the party, which is formed on the basis of voluntary adhesions to a common combat and sacrifice trench, these individual manifestations must remain rare exceptions and can be easily resolved.

But if these manifestations multiply and grow instead of decreasing and tending to disappear it means that something is wrong with the complex activity of the party and its central management; if only for the fact that instead of attracting healthy individuals who are willing to get rid of their individualistic itches, it begins to attract big mouths and fools. And this too is resolved not only in chasing chatterboxes, but in seeking the causes for which the organ party attracts them, and the remedy lies in making the party's appearance so sharp and clear in all its theoretical and practical manifestations as to discouraging any adhesion other than those who are willing to become a true militant of the revolution.

The solution never lies, for the Left, in intensifying bureaucratic barbed wire and organizational repression, which, as we always stated, we can gladly renounce, just as we can manage without the count of individual heads.

"The art of predicting how the party will react to orders, and which orders will obtain a good response, is the art of revolutionary tactics: this can only be entrusted to the collective use of the experience gained from past action, summarized in clear rules of action… Given that the party is perfectible and not perfect, we do not hesitate to say that much has to be sacrificed to the clarity and to the power of persuasion of the tactical guidelines, even if this involves a certain schematization…It is not just the good party that makes good tactics, but good tactics that make the good party, and good tactics can only be those understood and chosen by everyone in their fundamentals" (Draft Theses presented by the Left at the IIIrd Congress of P.C.d'I., Lyon 1926).

The guarantee of obedience to central orders by the base is no longer given by the observance of the articles of a statute or a code, but because they are those expected, since they belong to the common heritage of the party. The party hierarchy no longer needs to be elected by the base, nor to be nominated from above, because the only selection criterion remains that of the capacity to carry out the various functions of the party organ. That at the center there is a certain comrade rather than another cannot change anything in the political direction of the party, nor in its tactics; it can influence the greater or lesser central efficiency, but the designation of the most suitable militants in the various functions becomes a "natural and spontaneous" fact that does not need any particular sanction.

The party is a "voluntary" organization, not in the sense that it is adhered to by free rational choice, which we deny, but in the sense that every militant *"is materially free to leave us when he wants"* and that *"not even after the revolution we conceive forced access in our ranks"*. When you are in the organization you are required to observe the strictest discipline in the execution of central orders, but the transgression of this rule cannot be eliminated by the center except through the expulsion of the offenders. The center does not have available, in order to be obeyed, any other material sanctions.

What can keep the militant on the front line and make him loyal and obedient to the orders he receives? Certainly not the impositions of these orders, but the acknowledgement that they belong to that common ground, are consistent with the principles, aims, program, and action plan to which he adhered. Inasmuch as the party organ knows how to move on this historical basis, how to acquire it, how to permeate of it all its organization and its activity, the real conditions for the existence of the most absolute discipline can be set. To the extent that this occurs the cases of indiscipline, not attributable to individual issues, become less frequent and the party acquires a univocal behavior in action. The work to create a truly centralized organization, capable of responding at all times to unified provisions, therefore consists essentially in the continuous clarification and sculpting of the cornerstones of theory, program, tactics, and in the continuous conforming to them of the party's action, of its methods of struggle.

"…we must have an absolutely

homogeneous communist party, without differences of opinion and different groupings *within it. But this statement is not a dogma, it isn't an a priori principle; it is an end for which we can and must fight, in the course of development which will lead to the formation of the true communist party*, on condition, that is, that all ideological, tactical and organizational questions have been correctly posed and resolved… *Discipline then is* a point of arrival, not a point of departure, *not a platform that is somehow* indestructible. *Moreover, this corresponds to the voluntary nature of entry into our organization. So the remedy for the frequent cases of lack of discipline cannot be sought in some kind of party* penal code." (Report of the Left at the Fifth

Session of the Sixth Enlarged Executive of the Communist International, 23/2/1926).

Nor can be considered to be a sound remedy all measures of ideological and organizational terror, which recall the gloomy practices of Stalinism, destroyer of the party.

"Another lesson we can draw from events in the life of the Third International … is that of the vanity of "ideological terror", a horrible method in which it was attempted to substitute the natural process of diffusing our doctrine's via contact with harsh reality in a social setting, with forced indoctrination of recalcitrant and confused elements, either for reasons more powerful than party and humans or due to a faulty evolution of the party itself, by humiliating them and mortifying them in public congresses open even to the enemy, even if they had been leaders and exponents of party action during important political and historical episodes… Within the revolutionary party, as it moves inexorably towards victory, obeying orders is spontaneous and complete but not blind or compulsory. In fact, centralized discipline, as illustrated in our theses and associated supporting documentation, is equivalent to a perfect harmony of the duties and actions of the rank-and-file with those of the center, and the bureaucratic practices of an anti-Marxist voluntarism are no substitute for this.." (Supplementary theses on the historical task, the action and the structure of the world communist party, 1966).

"The party that we are sure to see resurrected in a bright future will be constituted by a vigorous minority of anonymous proletarians and revolutionaries, who may have different functions such as the organs of the same living being, but all will be linked, at the center and at the base, to the norm that is above all members, inflexible, of respect of theory; of continuity and rigor in organization; of a precise method of strategic action whose range of allowed eventualities is drawn, in its inviolable vetoes, from the terrible historical lesson of the ravages of opportunism. In such a party, at last impersonal, no one will be able to abuse power, precisely because of its unimitable characteristic, which distinguishes it in the uninterrupted thread that originated in 1848." (The theory of the primary function of the political party, only custody and salvation of the historical energy of the proletariat), Programma Comunista n. 21-22, 1958).

46. How to Spread the Duties

Already in 1924 we had pinpointed the role of the individual in the party: *"The organization in the party, which allows the class to be truly such and live as such, presents itself as a unitary mechanism in which the various" brains "(not only certainly the brains , but also other individual organs) perform different tasks according to their attitudes and potential, all at the service of a purpose and an interest that progressively unites itself more and more intimately "in time and space" (this convenient expression has an empirical and not transcendent meaning).*

Not all individuals therefore have the same place and the same weight in the organization: as this division of tasks is implemented according to a more rational plan (and what is today for the party-class will be tomorrow for society) is perfectly excluded that whoever finds himself higher is as privileged over others. Our revolutionary evolution does not go towards disintegration, but towards the increasingly scientific connection of individuals to each other.

It is anti-individualist since it is materialist; does not believe in the soul or in a metaphysical and transcendent content of the individual, but inserts the functions of this in a collective framework, creating a hierarchy that develops in the sense of increasingly eliminating coercion and replacing it with technical rationality. The party is already an example of a collective body without coercion.

These general elements of the question show that no one better than us is beyond the banal meaning of egalitarianism and "numerical" democracy ... In conclusion, if man, the "instrument", of exception exists, the movement uses it: but the movement lives the same when such an eminent personality is not found. " (Lenin on the path of revolution, 1924)

Assuming that the doctrine is not to be discussed, that the program is not discussed, that there is no discussion on the fundamental aspects of the tactical plan, the internal relations take the form of solidary and common work of all members of the party, aiming at finding, on the basis of an heritage common to all, the most appropriate solutions to the various problems.

From all this ensues the importance of common work; all comrades must work, this is obvious, but as far as possible the comrades should work in all areas, there must be no specializations, separations between those who do a certain job and those who do another, even if it is obvious that we are not identical, as we will not be even in full communism.

"The whole art of running a secret organization should consist in making use of everything possible, in "giving everyone something to do," at the same time retaining leadership of the whole movement, not by virtue of having the power, of course, but by virtue of authority, energy, greater experience, greater versatility, and greater talent." (VI, 240).

47. Impersonality and Anonymity

Joint work is the fulcrum of the organic nature of work in the party; the comrades approach their work free of any personalist, careerist attitude. In Lenin's time it was not possible, but since 1952 we have never published the names of the comrades who write reports, articles, theses. This is not a moral or aesthetical choice, it corresponds to the undeniable fact that ur work is no longer individual, if only because any study cannot ignore what is in our doctrine, what was previously written by other comrades, nor their past activity, whether these are the great Marx and Lenin or obscure comrades who have contributed for a day, a year or an entire life; even comrades who eventually abandoned the party and Marxism, to whom some of the quotations we have listed belong. The revolution, we wrote, will rise again, but anonymous. On the fact that our mission is above any individual Lenin makes Comrade Rusov talk:

""*We are hearing strange speeches from the lips of revolutionaries," Comrade Rusov justly remarked, "speeches that are in marked disharmony with the concepts Party work, Party ethics. The principal argument on which the opponents of electing trios take their stand amounts to* a purely philistine view of Party affairs" *[my italics throughout]....* "If we adopt this standpoint, which is *a philistine and not a Party standpoint, we shall at every election have to consider: will not Petrov be offended if Ivanov is elected and not he, will not some member of the Organizing Committee be offended if another member, and not he, is elected to the Central Committee? Where is this going to land us, comrades? If we have gathered here for the purpose of creating a Party, and* not of indulging in mutual compliments and philistine sentimentality, *then we can never agree to such a view. We are about to* elect officials, *and there can be no talk of lack of confidence in any person not elected;* our only consideration should be the interests of the work and a person's suitability for the post to which he is being elected"" (VII, 312-313).

Although, as mentioned above, it was not possible for Lenin to write anonymously at a time when he himself embodied Marxist doctrine, and his party was not entirely homogeneous in theory, he nevertheless shied away from any cult of his person, as can be seen from various testimonies, such as Andreev's ("Lénine comme il fut", 1958): "*Neither at meetings, nor at conferences, nor in the press, Lenin tolerated any praise, no exaltation of his personal merits; he opposed the cult of personality, alien to the Marxists, and always sincerely indignant at its minimal manifestations. The party and the masses always placed themselves in the foreground when analyzing historical events or tasks to be performed. Lenin's extreme modesty manifested itself in everything and always.*" Here it is easy to make the parallel with our greatest masters.

48. The False Solution of Expulsions

Organic centralism excludes the birth of fractions. By now the activity of a healthy party does not require, and therefore does not justify, the constitution of fractions that compete for its direction. Just as it is a symptom of serious malaise that on the periphery fractions are formed for the conquest of party leadership, so is the fact that the center conceives itself as a fraction, among whose functions there would be the maintenance of its office.

The birth of fractions, which in the old socialist parties could be a necessary and often useful fact when generated by movements in defense of Marxism, and therefore progressive in the evolution of the historical party, is, when it occurs in today's party, a pathological phenomenon; and this especially when the fraction that moves away from the just revolutionary policy is the one that belongs to the center, as happened in 1972-1973. Following this event, a group of comrades, who then continued on the correct path and who are now part of the International Communist Party, were expelled in 1973 by the organization of the time. Historically, as we have always said, it was the fraction of the center that left the party (from the historical party, while the formal one went towards an inevitable degeneration).

In 1972 the comrades of the Florence section wrote a letter to the center, relating to the expulsion of an entire foreign section, which we report because it provides further important clarifications on what organic centralism is: "... *It doesn't matter which comrade or group of comrades is at a given time, or on a given problem, in this or that of the two sides. It's the two sides that must never exist within the party. It is the way of life of the party that is based precisely on the absolute denial that sides exist and that one must fight against the other. If a single comrade or a group of comrades do not realize a situation or a problem or persist in an error, the whole party is committed to clarifying, sculpting, reiterating an impersonal line as the weakness of a party point is the weakness of the whole party, the lack of clarity of the whole organization. And we have always said that if a comrade does not have clear ideas, it means that the party has not worked hard enough to clarify them, that more work is needed by the whole party. This is the only way the party can live and function ... This is the organic method that is ours and that we claim, because it is the only method that allows us to live as an organization where there are neither comrades who understand, nor others who do not understand, neither comrades who make mistakes, nor others who do not make mistakes, but there are only comrades who, for better or worse, bring their contribution to the common battle against the class enemy and give this battle all their strength.*

For this reason, we do not share the triumphalist tone and statements of the last circular in which it is stated that the last general meeting ended the battle against the onset of anti-Marxist ideologies, etc. The anti-Marxist tendencies have been there, it is clear, but the emphasis should be placed not so much on the victory achieved when we managed to eliminate them from the party, but on the defeat we suffered when they managed to penetrate our interior, destroying precious energies and demolishing a part of our organization. We must certainly not congratulate ourselves on having expelled them, we should rather reflect on why they managed to penetrate our interior, and work to make the party stronger and more impervious to these destructive influences. We must judge that our defenses were too weak to prevent the enemy from dismantling them and working to strengthen these defenses. This is the lesson we must learn from the crisis that the party has suffered.''

Yet the party's attitude towards the fractions was clear since 1926, and continually reaffirmed in the theses:

"To raise the problem of fractions as a moral problem, from the point of view of a penal code is not the correct line of action. Is there any example in history of a comrade forming a fraction for his own amusement? Such a thing has never happened. Is there a historical example of opportunism insinuating itself into the party through a fraction, of the organisation of fractions serving as the basis for a defeatist mobilisation of the working class and of the revolutionary party being saved thanks to the intervention of the fraction-killers? No. Experience has shown that opportunism always infiltrates our ranks under the guise of unity. It is in its interest to influence the largest possible mass, and it is therefore behind the screen of unity that it puts forward its most deceitful proposals. Moreover, the history of fractions goes to show that if fractions do no honor to the parties in which they have been formed, they do honor to those who formed them ... The birth of a fraction shows that something has gone wrong in the party. To remedy the ill, it is necessary to seek out the historical causes which

gave rise to it, that gave rise to the fraction and that prompted it to take shape. The causes lie in the ideological and political errors of the party. The fractions are not the sickness, but merely the symptom, and if you want to treat a sick organism, you have to try to discover the causes of the sickness, not combat the symptoms" ("Report of the Left at the Fifth Session of the Sixth Enlarged Executive of the Communist International", 23 February 1926).

The lessons of defeats caused by the degeneration of the center are those that have strengthened us most, in the application of organic centralism. And those are the most painful, most disastrous defeats for the party. From the defeat of the parties of the Second International to that of the Moscow center, which would destroy the international revolutionary thrust in order to shackle the workers' movements to the interests of the Russian state.

49. Party and Fractions

The Left never hesitated to expound with the utmost frankness the objections that the behaviour of the center caused. It was so in the Italian Socialist Party; it was so in the International and even before Stalin himself. When the comrades of the Left were forced in 1925 to dissolve the Intesa Committee, they obeyed, but declared:

"In the face of a material imposition, we remember above all to stay at our post as soldiers of

*the Communist Party and of the International,
which we will maintain with an iron will, without
ever renouncing opposition, through tireless
criticism, of those methods that we consider to be in
conflict with the interest and the future of our
cause"* ("Un documento indegno di comunisti"
L'Unità, 18 July 1925).

In "The Opportunist Danger and the
International" (Stato Operaio, July 1925) we wrote,
without diplomacy:

*"We believe in the possibility that the
International will fall into opportunism ... The most
glorious and brilliant historical precedents cannot
guarantee a movement, even and above all a
revolutionary vanguard movement, against the
possibility of internal revisionism. The guarantees
against opportunism cannot consist in the past but
must be present and timely at all times.*

*"We do not see serious inconveniences in an
exaggerated concern for the opportunist danger. Of
course the criticism and alarmism made for fun are
very regrettable, but... it is certain that they will
have no means to weaken the movement in any way
and will be easily overcome. While the danger is
very serious if, on the contrary, as unfortunately
happened in so many precedents, the opportunist
disease is growing before one has dared somewhere
to vigorously give the alarm. Criticism without error
does not cause even one thousandth of the harm
caused by error without criticism.*

*"Comrade Girone puts the question in a simple
and clear way when he says that everything the*

leaders of the International say and do is a matter for which we claim the right to discuss, and to discuss means being able to doubt that something has been said and done wrong, regardless of any prerogative attributed to groups, humans and parties. Is it a question of repeating the holy apologia of freedom of thought and criticism as the right of the individual? No, of course, it is a question of establishing the physiological way of functioning and working of a revolutionary party, which must conquer, not preserve achievements of the past, invade the territories of the enemy, not close off its own with trenches and cordons sanitaires".

Therefore, to avoid splits and fractions, and even the mere loss of individual militants, the party has at its disposal the only instrument of the right revolutionary policy, the only physiological activity to prevent degeneration. And then back to the work of study, sculpting, clarification and demonstration of the rightness of the programmatic bases. Incidentally, nothing prevents the comrades who are the bearers of misunderstandings of our doctrine from participating in the work of clarification, of sculpting those aspects that require greater clarity. A process that also holds the secret to obtaining a correct response to orders, and also to the lack of orders, when the comrade must act without being able to discuss these with the party organs.

50. Anticipation of Future Society

A party therefore exists in that it defends not just the perspective of a communist future, but also a doctrine (theorisation and systematisation of the peculiar characteristics, collective interests and historical and immediate tasks of the class) and a method of operating (i.e., political activity and organisation of the struggle). For us, the party has always been a synthesis of a school of thought and a method of action.

All this is irrespective of the size the party has at a given historical moment, be it as number of members or geographical extent.

"Even accepting the party's restricted dimensions, we must realise that we are preparing the true party, sound and efficient at the same time, for the momentous period in which the infamies of the contemporary social fabric will compel the insurgent masses to return to the vanguard of history; a resurgence that could once again fail if there is no party; a party that is compact and powerful, rather than inflated in numbers, the indispensable organ of the revolution. Painful as the contradictions of this period are, they can be overcome by drawing the dialectical lessons from the bitter disappointments of times past, and by courageously signalling the dangers that the Left warned about, and denounced as they appeared, along with all the insidious forms in which the

ominous opportunist infection reveals itself time and time again" ("Supplementary Theses on the Historical task, the Action and the Structure of the World Communist Party", 1966).

As a conclusion, one should not think that the party looks like a traditional army unit, in which every behaviour and statement is looked upon with suspicion and subjected to stringent controls. Nor is the party *"a phalanstery surrounded by impassable walls"*, suspicious of external contamination, which in reality cannot be avoided, if for no other reason than the succession of comrades of a thousand origins, and of generations with different backgrounds and experiences. In reality the common work, and the common goal, make comrades linked by "fraternal consideration"; in the party there is a tendency to give life to a strongly anti-bourgeois environment, which, despite the conditioning due to the immersion in this inhuman society, determines an anticipation of the characteristics of the future communist society. The party as *"anticipation of the future society"* is the synthesis of what a militant feels and lives, while he offers his life to that great upheaval of human history that will make humanity leap, in Engels' meaning, from the kingdom of necessity to the kingdom of freedom.

"…to raise the problem of fractions as a moral problem, from the point of view of a penal code is not the correct line of action. Is there any example in history of a comrade forming a fraction for his own amusement? *Such a thing has never happened. Is there a historical example of opportunism*

insinuating itself into the party through a fraction, of the organization of fractions serving as the basis for a defeatist mobilization of the working class and of the revolutionary party being saved thanks to the intervention of the fraction-killers? No. Experience has shown that opportunism always infiltrates our ranks under the guise of unity. It is in its interest to influence the largest possible mass, and it is therefore behind the screen of unity that it puts forward its most deceitful proposals. Moreover, the history of fractions goes to show that if fractions do no honor to the Parties in which they have been formed, they do honor to those who formed them. ... The birth of a fraction shows that something has gone wrong in the party. To remedy the ill, it is necessary to seek out the historical causes which gave rise to it, that gave rise to the fraction and that prompted it to take shape. The causes lie in the ideological and political errors of the party. *The fractions are not the sickness, but merely the symptom, and if you want to treat a sick organism, you have to try to discover the causes of the sickness, not combat the symptoms.* " (Report of the Left at the Fifth Session of the Sixth Enlarged Executive of the Communist International, 23/2/1926).

The lessons of defeats caused by the degeneration of the center are those that have strengthened us most, in the application of organic centralism. And those are the most painful, most disastrous defeats for the party. From the one of the Second International parties to that of the center of

Moscow, which would destroy the international revolutionary drive to enslave the workers' movements to the interests of the Russian state.

49. Party and fractions

The Left never hesitated to expound with the utmost frankness the objections that the behavior of the center caused. So it was in the Italian Socialist Party, so it was in the International and before Stalin himself. When the comrades of the Left were forced in 1925 to dissolve the Intesa Committee, they obeyed, but declaring: "*In the light of a material imposition we remember to hold especially in our place as gregarious of the communist party and of the International, which we will keep with iron will, but without ever giving up a tireless criticism of those methods that we consider conflicting with the interest and the future of our cause.*" ("*Un documento indegno di comunisti*" *L'Unità*, July 18, 1925)

In "The opportunist danger and the International" (Stato Operaio, July 1925) we wrote, without diplomacy: "*We believe in the possibility that the International will fall into opportunism … The most glorious and brilliant historical precedents cannot guarantee a movement, even and above all a revolutionary avant-garde movement, against the possibility of internal revisionism. The guarantees against opportunism cannot consist in the past, but must be present and timely at all times.*

We do not see serious inconveniences in an exaggerated concern for the opportunist danger. Of course the criticism and alarmism made for fun are very regrettable, but ... it is certain that they will have no way to weaken the movement in any way, and will be easily overcome. While the danger is very serious if, on the contrary, as unfortunately happened in so many precedents, the opportunist disease is growing before one has dared somewhere to vigorously give the alarm. Criticism without error does not harm even the thousandth part of the damage caused by the error without criticism.

... Comrade Girone puts the question in a simple and clear way when he says that everything the leaders of the International say and do is a matter of which we claim the right to discuss, and to argue means to be able to doubt that something has been said and done wrong, regardless of any prerogative attributed to groups, humans and parties. Is it a question of repeating the holy apology of freedom of thought and criticism as the right of the individual? No, of course, it is a question of establishing the physiological way of functioning and working of a revolutionary party, which must conquer, not preserve achievements of the past, invade the territories of the enemy, not close its own with trenches and quarantine lines."

Therefore, to avoid splits and fractions, and even just the loss of individual militants, the party has at its disposal the only instrument of the right revolutionary policy, the only *physiological* activity to prevent degeneration. And then back to the work of study, sculpting, clarification and demonstration of the rightness of the programmatic bases. Incidentally, nothing prevents the comrades who are the bearers of misunderstandings of our doctrine from participating in the work of clarification, of sculpting those aspects that require greater clarity.

A work that is also the secret to get a correct answer to orders, and also to the lack of orders, when the comrade must act without being able to relate to the party organs.

50. Anticipation of future society

A party therefore that exists in that it defends not just the perspective of a communist future, but also a doctrine (theorization and systematization of the peculiar characteristics, collective interests and historical and immediate tasks of the class) and a method of operating (i.e., political activity and organization of the struggle). For us, the party has always been a synthesis of a school of thought and a method of action.

All this irrespective of the size the party has in a given historical moment, be it as number of members or geographical extension. *"Even accepting the party's restricted dimensions, we must realize that we are preparing the true party, sound and efficient at the same time, for the momentous period in which the infamies of the contemporary social fabric will compel the insurgent masses to*

*return to the vanguard of history; a resurgence that
could once again fail if there is no party; a party
that is compact and powerful, rather than inflated in
numbers, the indispensable organ of the revolution.
Painful as the contradictions of this period are, they
can be overcome by drawing the dialectical lessons
from the bitter disappointments of times past, and by
courageously signalling the dangers that the Left
warned about, and denounced as they appeared,
along with all the insidious forms in which the
ominous opportunist infection reveals itself time and
time again."* (Supplementary Theses on the
historical task, the action and the structure of the
World Communist Party, 1966).

As a conclusion, one should not think that the
party looks like a traditional army unit, in which
every behavior and statement are looked upon with
suspicion and subjected to stringent controls. Nor is
the party "*a phalanstery surrounded by impassable
walls*", suspicious of external contamination, which
in reality cannot be avoided, if for no other reason
than the succession of comrades of a thousand
origins, and of generations with different
backgrounds and experiences. In reality the common
work, and the common goal, make the comrades
linked by "fraternal consideration"; in the party there
is a tendency to give life to a strongly anti-bourgeois
environment, which, despite the conditioning due to
the immersion in this inhuman society, determines
an anticipation of the characteristics of the future
communist society. The party "*anticipation of the
future society*" is the synthesis of what a militant

feels and lives, while he offers his life to that great upheaval of human history that will make humanity leap, in Engels' meaning, from the kingdom of necessity to the kingdom of freedom.